Freeform
Knitting and
Crochet

Freeform
Knitting and Crochet

Jenny Dowde

SALLY MILNER
PUBLISHING

Dedication

For my mother Joan Halloran-Turner

My best friend…

She would have been so very proud…

First published in 2004 by
Sally Milner Publishing Pty Ltd
PO Box 2104
Bowral NSW 2576
AUSTRALIA

© Jenny Dowde 2004

Design: Anna Warren, Warren Ventures
Editing: Bridging the Gap
Photography: Tim Connolly
Illustrations: Anna Warren, Warren Ventures

Printed in China

National Library of Australia Cataloguing-in-Publication data

Dowde, Jenny.
  Freeform knitting and crochet.
  ISBN 1 86351 327 2.
  1. Knitting. 2. Crocheting. I. Title. (Series : Milner craft series).
  746.43

Disclaimer
The information in this instruction book is presented in good faith. However, no warranty is given, nor results guaranteed, nor is freedom from any patent to be inferred. Since we have no control over the use of the information contained in this book, the publisher and the author disclaim liability for untoward results.

10 9 8 7 6 5 4 3 2 1

Contents

Acknowledgements

An author must have a starting point before commencing to write a book and the starting point for this book was, in the first place, a simple desire to share what so many people have inspired me to discover over the years. They are too numerous to name individually, but among them are my art teachers who 'taught me to see', my students who never fail to teach me something and all artists since time began, all of whom have added something to the creative mix.

Those I do want to thank by name are:

- Chris and Paul who put up with a lot but who were always there…

- James Walters and Sylvia Cosh who started me on this amazing freeform journey…

- Paul Higgs who taught me all about colour…

- Kurt M. Fowler whose humour kept me sane through the whole process of putting this book together and whose belief in me is unwavering…

- Kristen Dibbs who, along with James Walters, encouraged, advised and more than anything else, understood!

- Sue Bennett who urged me to 'keep at it' when I was ready to admit defeat…

- Gail McHugh who brought me down to earth when I needed it and nagged me incessantly…

- Lynne Johnson and Margaret Hubert who so generously contributed their talents…

- Alison Vincent who not only contributed her 'Scarf That Grew' and 'Zebra Bag' projects but who did all of the initial proofreading and test sampling. I cannot thank her enough!

- Judy Harris who had faith enough to make the prediction back in 1993…

- The staff at Sally Milner Publishing who gave me this incredible opportunity by accepting my manuscript and who answered all the dumb questions without making me feel dumb…

- Alison, Bonnie, Cris, Lynne and Robyn for allowing me to show their work in the Gallery, and Melba for lending me 'Tracks'. You were all so incredibly patient!

JENNY

About This Book

Since the main objective of this book is to introduce you to the wonderful world of 'Taking your yarn for a walk' through the mediums of colour, texture and freeform crochet and knitting (also known as 'scrumbling'), most of the projects are by design very straightforward with a low to medium degree of difficulty. While all of the more complex stitches are included in the 'Crochet Stitch Collection', 'FUNky FX' and 'How to' chapters, familiarity with basic crochet and knit stitches, such as chain stitch, double crochet (US sc), trebles (US dc), garter stitch, stocking stitch, etc., is necessary before you embark on the projects.

For those of you who like a challenge, once you have learned the techniques and understood the concept of scrumbling, or working in freeform manner, you will find it easy to adapt to larger projects and to the creation of wearable art.

Three very special people have graciously contributed their original ideas and I gratefully acknowledge their generosity and friendship: Lynne Johnson of Canberra, Alison Vincent of Sydney and Margaret Hubert from Pawling, New York. Each of these talented people 'takes their yarn for a walk' in their own unique way and I know you will enjoy their ideas and techniques.

It is my hope that the various chapters will inspire you to experiment, to create your own style and to always ask yourself 'What if?'

As my good friend, Kurt M. Fowler, once said:

'Onward, Dream Looper!'

JENNY DOWDE

'Taking Your Yarn for a Walk' –
The Technique of Scrumbling

'**T**aking your yarn for a walk' has been a favourite phrase of mine for some years and was inspired by the artist, Paul Klee, who once used the words 'taking a line for a walk' when talking about his painting and drawing. It so aptly describes scrumbling.

I first discovered the technique of scrumbling in 1997 when I attended a workshop called 'The Fabric of Landscape' held at Mittagong Textile Fibre Forum. The tutors were Sylvia Cosh and James Walters from the United Kingdom and they changed my creative life.

What is 'scrumbling'?

'*It is all about peeling off the layers of household grime which have accumulated around the infinitely popular, but limited, "painting by numbers" tradition of domestic crochet. It is a brilliantly simple and expressive technique: starting with a hook and a continuous thread of some kind, each of us can make fabrics and structures in two and three dimensions, allowing our eyes, hands and heart all to work together to create intuitively and immediately.*'

JAMES WALTERS

I had been a knit designer for many years, mainly machine knits, and I loved the immediacy of using a knitting machine as a creative tool for creating unique designs easily! I was never one for doing swatches; in fact, I hated making them and avoided it wherever possible. It was this that led to a design approach slightly less technical than the norm.

Many of my designs, both of necessity and by preference, evolved on the machine. It was impossible to adhere to the original design idea because more often than not the lack of a swatch and therefore the lack of a stitch gauge meant that my garments were usually too small. It was inevitable, therefore, that I began to think outside the square and this grew to be a wonderfully liberating experience. It mattered not in the least that a jacket was too short or too narrow. Adding a contrasting yoke or panels soon fixed this, and I found that by throwing the rules out the window I could create wonderful wearables that were even more unusual than the original idea — and without having to follow a pattern!

I have given this approach to making garments the title 'Grow As You Go' and you can read about it at the end of the 'Putting It All Together' chapter.

Scrumbling is like that. It offers total design freedom, and for me this is the most compelling characteristic of the technique. You need only the basics of crochet to scrumble. Chains, double crochet (US sc), trebles (US dc), etc. — these form the basis of all the textured stitches. And since you don't have to follow rules or patterns, or worry about the edges being even and so on, you don't ever need to worry about the technical side of crochet.

While my introduction to scrumbling came through the medium of crochet, I have for some time now been scrumbling with my knitting needles as well, just as I once did on my knitting machine. Once again, you can throw out the rules and let your yarns and needles work for you. As with crochet, you really only need the basics — casting on, casting off, and knit and purl stitches! With knitted scrumbling you can use 'fragments', as discussed in 'Knit Fragments'; you can knit geometrical or amorphous shapes and scrumble over the top; or you can just start knitting and let the yarn and needles take you where they will.

Although total design freedom is the key factor in scrumbling, I have discovered in my workshops that the concept is not always obvious to the learner. Therefore, it is hoped that this book will help bridge the gap between the technical side of knitting and crochet and the design freedom of the scrumbling technique by means of simple patterns for what I call 'fragments'. Once the concept has been understood, your creative spirit will be free to soar and explore to its heart's content.

Colour

'Color possesses me. There is no need to seize it. It possesses me. I know. Here is the meaning of the happy moment: color and I are one. I am a painter.'

PAUL KLEE

Colour is my passion! Not only is it the most exciting design element, it is also the most important and the most complex! How we use colour can determine the success or failure of a design.

Very few of us were born with an intuitive colour sense; most of us have learned to be intuitive after years of either working with or observing colour in the environment that surrounds us. Combining colours successfully can be a huge challenge, especially for someone new to it. Many artists, when learning to paint, are overwhelmed by the enormity of colour theory and the importance of interpreting it successfully in their art. The same can be said of textile artists, particularly when learning a new technique, such as scrumbling, where so many colours may be used in any one project.

Unfortunately, we are conditioned by outside influences as we grow up. As children, we used colour freely and without inhibition. It didn't matter if the tree we painted was blue and the grass was orange; at the time we painted it, we wanted that tree to be blue and the grass orange, and so we painted what was in our hearts. Because we once worked so freely with colour, we are all capable of recapturing that childhood magic. It's just a matter of reaching down inside your 'self' and finding that wonderful freedom once more. It might take a little time and a lot of experimenting but it will be well worth the effort.

To begin your journey, take a trip to your local library and borrow some books on colour (see 'Bibliography'). There is a wonderful book called Intertidal Wilderness by Ann Wertheim that has some unbelievably beautiful imagery in it and it's well worth trying to locate a copy for your own collection of inspirational books. Look at the art of Cézanne, Klee, Kandinsky, Monet and Van Gogh, to name a few. Surf the Internet for sites that deal with colour. Check out rocks and crystals: the colours in some of these are breathtaking! Take a walk around your garden and really see what you are looking at. Notice that the leaves in the trees aren't just one shade of green! Look closely and you will see myriad shades of green, together with shades of red and yellow.

The basics of colour theory

'It is not quantity which counts [with colours], but choice and organization.'

HENRI MATISSE

Fig 1: Primary colours

There are a number of terms that you should familiarise yourself with when learning about colour.

PRIMARY COLOURS

Red, Yellow and Blue

SECONDARY COLOURS

These occur when any two primaries are mixed together, for example:

Red + Yellow = Orange

Blue + Yellow = Green

Red + Blue = Purple

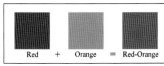

Fig 2: Secondary colours

TERTIARY COLOURS

These occur when any primary colour is combined with any secondary colour, for example:

Red + Orange = Red-Orange

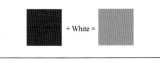

Fig 3: Tertiary colours

HUE

This refers to the pure colour with nothing added to lighten or darken it.

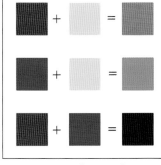

Fig 4: Tint

TINT

Any colour that has had white added to it.

SHADE

Any colour that has had black or another dark colour added to it.

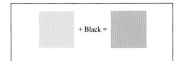

Fig 5: Shade

TONE OR VALUE

Every colour has a value, i.e. a specific degree of lightness or darkness. Perhaps the most important issue to consider when combining colours is the tonal value of each colour in relation to another. This more than anything else determines the success or failure of your colour choices. Changing the tonal value of a colour can cause a marked difference in how one colour interacts with another. When colours of the same tonal value are used together, they can become confusing and indistinguishable. Fig. 6, for example, shows that colours of similar tonal value lack visual impact. Fig. 7 shows how colours of different tonal value create a vibrant and more interesting colour scheme.

Using too many colours, or introducing colours that are tonally incorrect, can result in a colour scheme that has an unsettling effect on

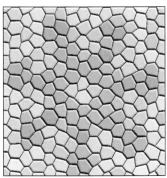

Fig. 6 Similar tonal value = insufficient contrast

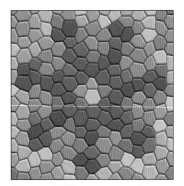

Fig. 7: Different tonal
values = contrast

Fig. 8

Fig. 9

the viewer (see Fig. 8). On the other hand, the colour scheme in Fig. 9 conveys a feeling of harmony and unity.

WARM COLOURS

This term describes colours such as red, yellow and orange and also includes red-violet. Warm colours have a tendency to move forward in a colour scheme.

COOL COLOURS

This term describes colours such as blues and greens and also includes violet. Cool colours have a tendency to recede in a colour scheme.

ACHROMATIC

'Achromatic' means 'without colour' and refers to black, greys and whites.

Using an achromatic colour scheme doesn't mean that your work will be boring. For example, in 'Homage to a Magpie' (see 'Gallery'), I combined both matte and shiny whites and blacks with soft silvery greys and the merest touches of soft blues and reds, and then added a little metallic yarn for some extra interest.

Fig. 10: Warm colours

Fig. 11: Cool colours

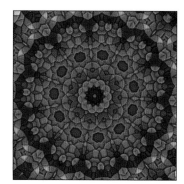

Fig. 12: Achromatic

MONOCHROMATIC

This refers to a scheme of one colour only plus its tints and shades.

HIGH KEY

A high-key colour scheme is one in which most or all of the colours are light or pale in value. Colours mixed with white, i.e. pastels or tints, are high key.

AVERAGE OR MEDIUM KEY

A medium-key colour scheme is one in which most or all of the colours sit somewhere between tints or shades.

Fig. 13: Monochromatic

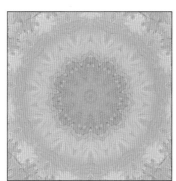

Fig. 14: High key

Fig. 15: Average or medium key

LOW KEY

A low-key colour scheme is one in which most or all of the colours are dark in value. Colours mixed with black, i.e. shades, are low key.

ANALOGOUS COLOURS

This refers to colours that are adjacent to a key colour with one colour in common. In the example in Fig. 17, red is the common colour.

Fig. 16: Low Key

Fig. 17: Analogous colours

COMPLEMENTARY COLOURS

These are colours that are directly opposite each other on the colour wheel, such as orange and blue, red and green, yellow and purple.

The relationship between these opposing colours and their effects is especially important. This is because the closer two colours approach a 'complementary relationship', the greater the stimulation to the eye. Each colour appears brighter against its complement than when standing alone in a neutral or weaker background, (Fig 18b).

Fig. 18a: Complementary colours

Fig. 18b: Complementary colours

SPLIT COMPLEMENTS

This refers to a key colour combined with the two colours that are next to its complement (see Figs 19 and 20).

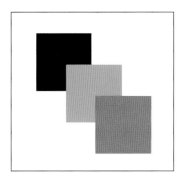

Fig. 19: Split complements
Key colour (purple) with the two colours that are next to its complement (yellow)

Fig. 20: Split complements

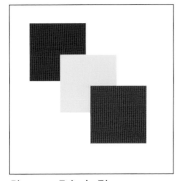

Fig. 21: Triad. Three colours equally spaced from each other

Fig. 21a: Triad

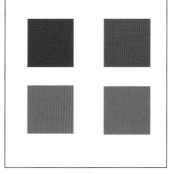

TRIADIC COLOUR SCHEME

This refers to three colours that are evenly and equally spaced from each other, forming a triangle.

TETRAD COLOUR SCHEME

A tetrad colour scheme is where four colours that are equidistant on a standard 12-part colour wheel form a square or rectangle.

Fig. 22: Tetrad. 4 colours that are equidistant on a colour wheel

Colour interaction

Colour interaction is a particularly significant aspect of colour theory. It refers to the way in which a colour appears to change when surrounded by different coloured backgrounds. In Figs 23 and 24 the same quantity of identical red has been placed on a blue background and a green background. You will see that the red seems to have been modified. This effect is known as simultaneous contrast — the increase or decrease in intensity of a colour when seen in proximity to other colours — and is discussed in depth in Patricia Lambert's book, *Color and Fiber* and other books on colour (see 'Bibliography').

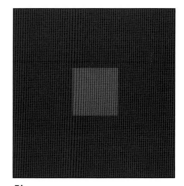

Fig. 23

Tips for livening up a colour scheme

By making colours fractionally lighter or darker we can upset the natural tonal order of colour to achieve more interesting colour combinations. This is called colour discord and these lightened colours can be used as accents to liven up a pleasant but otherwise dull scheme. For example, in a predominately red/orange combination, since red is generally considered to be darker than orange you would lighten the red to pink and use this pink in small amounts to add vibrancy to the scheme. Or you would use small amounts of pale violet against dark green or light blue against deep red.

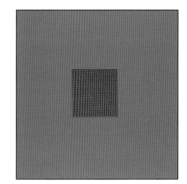

Fig. 24

Fig. 25

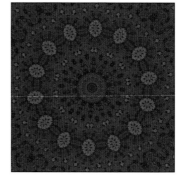

Fig. 26

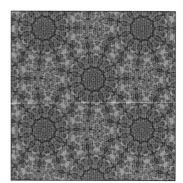

Fig. 27

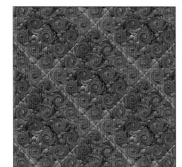

Fig. 28

USING MORE THAN ONE ACCENT COLOUR

In larger projects you may need to add more than one accent. For example, in a predominately blue/green combination, try adding flashes of yellow, pink and orange.

If another colour doesn't seem to solve the problem, the careful addition of black and white may work. This can be extremely effective, but do be wary of using too much of either colour. In this particular case, less is definitely more.

USING COMPLEMENTARY COLOURS

The colours opposite each other on the colour wheel exert the greatest change, or reaction, to each other and create the greatest intensity. To add vibrancy to a colour scheme try combining orange against blue, red against green and yellow against purple.

Fig. 29

Fig. 30

Fig. 31

Fig. 32

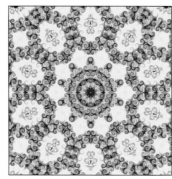

Fig. 33

Fig. 34

USING A COLOUR WHEEL

'Remember, objectively there is really no such thing as a "bad"
colour scheme. Taste really is a matter of personal preference.'

UNKNOWN

Putting a little time and effort into learning colour theory can have a very positive effect on your work (see 'Bibliography' for further reading suggestions). If you are new to or unsure of how to use colour, buy an artist's colour wheel, as it is probably one of the most useful things you can have in your toolbox. You can find them at art supply shops for around $20 for the large size, and it really is money well spent. Figs. 35a and 35b show the front and reverse of a colour wheel.

The information on the wheel includes explanations of key terminology, as discussed above, including definitions of primary colours, secondary colours, tertiary colours and complementary colours. It is constructed to allow you to immediately see various colour combinations, such as triadic and analogous colour schemes.

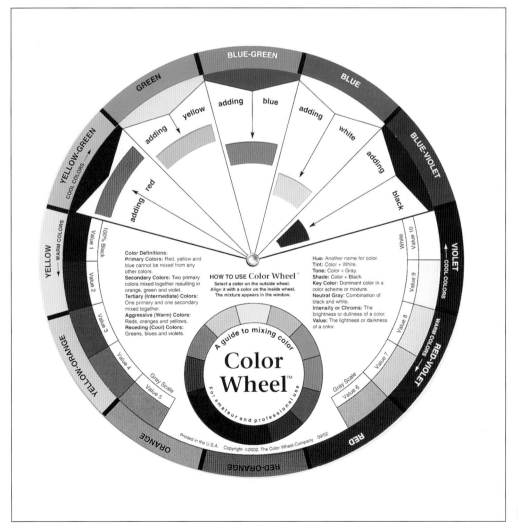

Fig. 35a

Fig. 35b

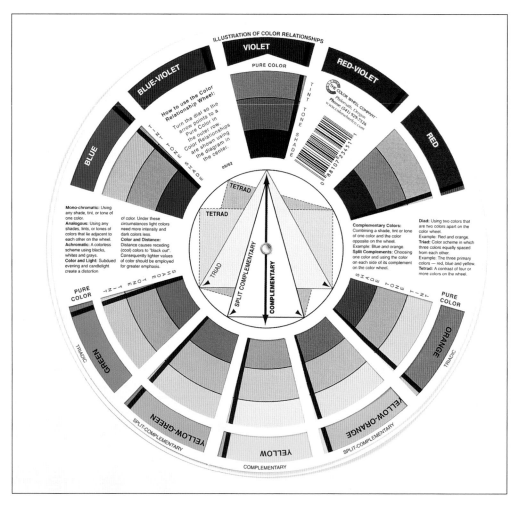

Developing a colour scheme

'Developing a sensitivity to [colour] value relationships should be the aim of all designers/artists.'

UNKNOWN

Tip: When using a colour wheel to help develop a colour scheme based on a given colour, it is important to consider all its shades and tints and to refer to your yarn stash and include any shades and tints you find there as well.

A colour scheme refers to the colours selected for a particular design. It is worth noting at this point that a group of colours that work well together in one design may not be as successful in another. This is because the positions of the colours, the size of the colour areas and the effects of contrasts must all be considered. In other words, you must achieve colour balance. Using colours together skilfully allows the designer to exploit the language of colour to the full. In order to achieve this, you should be willing to experiment constantly and expect sometimes to fail! Failure means that you learn something; constant success means that you run the risk of becoming complacent.

COLOUR INSPIRATIONS

The obvious place to start looking for colour combinations is in nature. We are surrounded by colour every day and it will really help you to start 'seeing' your surroundings. Other elements to consider are fabrics — a favourite skirt or dress perhaps.

Study the work of Kaffe Fassett. He is a master colourist who uses easily accessed sources, such as stone walls, vegetation and landscapes, as colour inspiration. Look through your own photographs, as well as those in magazines, particularly publications such as National Geographic.

Fig. 36 shows a photograph of a sunset that was used as inspiration for the 'Red Sky at Night' knitted bag (see Fig. 68 in 'Knit Fragments').

Fig. 36

COMPUTER SOFTWARE GENERATED COLOUR SCHEMES

While there is no substitute for learning as much as you can about colour theory from books and doing colour exercises of your own, there is no reason why you can't take short cuts to help you achieve your aims and have some fun at the same time.

If you have a computer, there are some very useful yet inexpensive programs available that will help you create colour scheme ideas. Some I have worked with are: Gliftic and Repligator, Color Schemer and Color Impact, see 'Resources'. Used separately, or in conjunction with one another, they will very quickly generate colour ideas for you to build on. (See 'Design' for more about Gliftic and Repligator.)

Both Color Impact and Color Schemer are wonderful little tools, originally intended to help Web designers create visually pleasing websites. However, they can be just as useful for textile artists, as you will see from the examples discussed below.

Fig. 37a

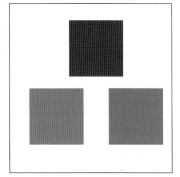

Fig. 37

COLOR IMPACT

The following diagrams illustrate just how easy it is to choose a base colour, either from a scanned image, an existing image or the inbuilt colour wheel in Color Impact, and then generate a colour scheme based on that colour using the program.

For my base colour I chose violet (purple). The scheme chosen from a drop-down menu containing 27 options was Triad. The other two colours in this particular Triadic selection were a blue-based green and a red-based yellow. This meant that on the colour wheel they were positioned closer to blue and red than to yellow.

I then generated 16 similar colours relating to those in Fig. 37, which gave me a palette of pure colours. Finally, I generated a palette each of tints and shades based on those 16 pure colours.

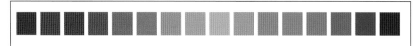

Fig. 38: Original palette of 16 colours

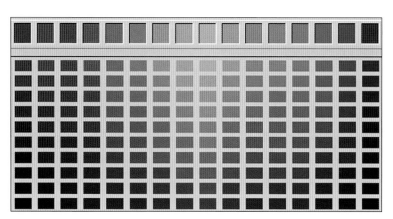

Fig. 39: Original palette of 16 colours including shades

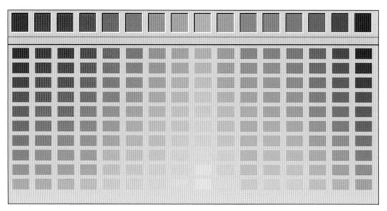

Fig. 40: Original palette of 16 colours including tints

From these selections I could then choose yarns from my stash that were within the range of the colours generated. Of course, you would not have exactly the same colours in your stash; however, careful selection from those yarns that did fall within this range would result in a perfectly harmonious colour scheme.

COLOR SCHEMER

When you first open Color Schemer, you are presented with a small screen that shows a group of 16 colours (see Fig. 41). You can choose others from a collection of included samples or click on a colour in the colour palette to generate a new one based on that colour.

As with Color Impact, you can use a scanned or existing image, or choose one of the in-built colour schemes as a starting point. Fig. 42 shows a scan of yarn used as the source for the colour scheme in Fig. 43.

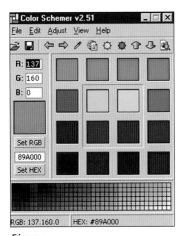

Fig.41

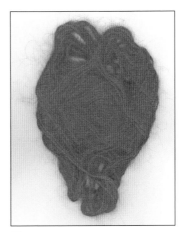

Fig.42

Fig.43

The ability to choose a colour from a scan or existing image opens up all kinds of possibilities for creating colour schemes from any source, including photographs, fabrics and paintings. Imagine a colour scheme based on a painting by a favourite artist (see Fig. 46), a child's painting or one of your own artworks (see Fig. 44)!

Fig.44: J Dowde, 'Landscape Series 1'

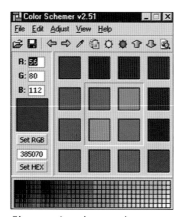

Fig.47

Fig.45: A colour scheme based on the painting in Fig. 44

It's just as easy to generate schemes based on artwork using Color Impact. Fig. 47 shows a scheme generated by Color Impact and based on the colours in Fig. 46.

RAIDING THE YARN STASH

Whether you use software to help you choose your colour scheme or are inspired by a painting, a photographic image or a gorgeous skein of variegated yarn, your job isn't finished yet. Your next step is to collect all the possibilities from your yarn stash, including all shades and tints of each colour chosen, and pile them onto a table in your studio, if you have one, or anywhere that you can leave them undisturbed for a few days. As you 'live' with the selection, you will find yourself removing yarns that do not 'feel' right. After a little time, these misfits will become reasonably obvious to you!

Regardless of how many yarns you remove from the grouping, there will be some that you won't reject until you've actually used them in your work. This shouldn't happen very often, but take heart from the fact that the 'experts' get it wrong now and again and find it necessary to reject a yarn in order to restore balance to their work.

Fig.46: Design inspired by 'Woman with Hat, Paris' Henri Matisse

Fig. 48: Monochromatic

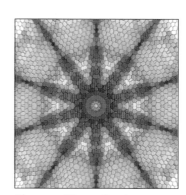

Fig. 49: Warm Cool

Fig. 50: Tetrad

A collection of colour schemes based on colour wheel theory

RECREATING YARNS

I expect that all of us at some time or other have purchased a yarn that makes us wonder a few months down the track why on earth we did so! Mostly they just end up sitting around taking up room or being given away. Not any more! There are things you can do to transform these yarns into ones that you will use.

Start by collecting all the yarns you think you won't ever use in their present state. Arrange them in their own colour groupings, as that will make it easier for you to analyse them. If some of them are very chunky, say a 12 to 14 ply (Heavy Worsted), it may not be possible to 'salvage' them, without resorting to overdyeing the yarns, so for now discard them. The success of this experiment does depend somewhat on having finer yarns to work with.

Perhaps you have an extremely bright orange colour that is just too vivid to use alone. By choosing a mustard tone of yellow and plying them together, it's possible that the orange will be toned down enough to use in small areas. If not, add two strands of the mustard and see how that works. You can do this with any of the bright colours, gradually adding strands of finer yarns until the brightness is suitably muted. The perfect yarns for doing this are some of the thinner coned machine knitting yarns, but of course not everyone will have these. Instead, you could try adding sewing threads to the thicker yarns. Work with the yarns you have but be aware that combining several thicker yarns will create a very chunky new yarn.

Tip: When toning down brights you should look for yarns with a tonal value that is lower than the yarn you are altering. For example:

- Bright red? Try combining with a moss or olive green, a darker red or even purple.

- Too blue? Combine with purples or a deep rusty orange, or several other shades of blue.

- Dull and boring? Add some zing by combining with a metallic thread or something textured, such as a fine bouclé.

Fig. 51

Fig. 52

Fig. 53

As you can see from the knitted samples in Figs 51, 52 and 53, the original yarn at the left of each sample was transformed into something much more interesting as each new yarn was added. Several of the variations in each example work rather well and are much more visually exciting than the original yarn.

I find that garter stitch or the purl side of stocking stitch fabric looks more interesting when using this technique; however, this is a personal choice. You could also experiment with moss stitch or blackberry stitch or any number of knit or crochet stitches.

All the 'added' yarns in the examples were normal plies (weights), from 4 ply (Fingering) to 8 ply (DK), and in order to avoid fabric that was too dense I changed the knitting needle size as I went. In my samples the red and yellow original yarns were 8 ply (DK) and the blue one was a chunky 10 ply (Worsted) yarn.

Since the recreated yarns do tend to be heavier, an ideal way to use them is to make garments or accessories using large gauge knitting needles or crochet hooks. Not only does this help create a fabric with some drape, it also makes for much speedier knitting or crocheting!

Tip: Try using the finer machine knitting yarns to recreate your own. Or if you prefer not to create chunky yarns, try adding sewing thread instead of yarn.

I cannot emphasise enough how important it is to experiment. As the words of the following quote indicate, experimenting need never be a chore!

' I never practise; I always play.'

WANDA LANDOWSKA

Design

'How can I qualify my faith in the inviolability of the design principles? Their virtue is demonstrated. They work.'

EDGAR WHITNEY

It is beyond the scope of this book to discuss the principles and elements of design in depth; however, an understanding of some of them at least is important in order to achieve good design. Should you wish to do further research after reading the brief discussion that follows the best place to begin is in the art section of your local library. The Internet is another very good resource, and there are many informative sites available for you to explore.

The principles of design are:

Contrast – Emphasis – Balance – Unity – Pattern – Movement – Rhythm

The elements of design are:

Colour – Line – Value – Shape and Form – Space – Texture

The important principles and elements to think about in freeform work are colour, contrast, unity, value and texture.

Colour

See chapter on 'Colour'.

Contrast

This refers to the contrast between textured areas and non-textured areas. Contrast in materials immediately brings to mind all the wonderful contrasting yarns available to us. While it is perfectly acceptable to use plain, smooth yarns in your freeform work, for me the combination of plain and fancy is much more visually exciting.

Unity

Unity means *harmony* and without it chaos can rule. Think about the textures you are using and take care to place them in a balanced way. Rather than slapping on a single circular motif just because you feel like it, think about *balancing* it by using similar elements elsewhere in your work.

If you choose to knit or crochet a plain back for a vest or plain sleeves for a jacket, it's a good idea to add some of the yarn used for them within the scrumbled areas as this will help tie the overall design together.

Balance or consistency is something that should always be considered, although if you achieve *unity* in your work, then *balance* should occur naturally.

Value

This was also discussed in the chapter on 'Colour' but it is worth discussing again as it is perhaps the most elusive of the design elements. Between the whitest white and the blackest black there are limitless degrees of light and dark values. Too many values used in combination can be confusing and result in a weak design. Within a range of values, such as light, medium and dark, you can find a useful variety. Colours that are close in value appear to merge together, for example, dark green and black. If you want more contrast, one of the chosen colours should be lighter in value, for example, dark green and mid grey.

Texture

Texture is the quality of a surface, whether it's smooth or rough, faded or bright, soft or hard. Scrumbling gives us the ultimate excuse for indulging our passion for this particular design element through the use of textured stitches and/or yarns.

Generating design ideas on the computer

As mentioned in the previous chapter, there is some wonderful, inexpensive software available that is fun to use and extremely useful for those moments when creativity abandons us, as it does from time to time.

GLIFTIC
This program allows you to create your own unique designs quickly, intuitively and easily.

Designs consist of three parts:

1. Form (the general layout of the image)

2. Colour scheme (how the image is coloured)

3. Interpretation (how the form is interpreted)

Gliftic allows you to create an image by quickly experimenting with these three components.

REPLIGATOR

With this program you can quickly create striking and original new images based on your own images. You start with an image (which you create in Gliftic or a paint program, or scan in) and apply effects to it. There is an internal Wizard, which can automatically select various settings for you, so that all you have to do is import an image and push F7 a few times. Nothing could be easier!

Examples of imagery generated by Gliftic and Repligator are included in Figs 54–60.

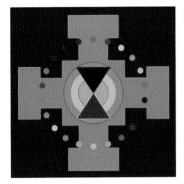

Fig 54: Gliftic image for symmetrical scrumbling

Fig. 55: Gliftic image for wire or lace work

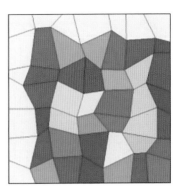

Fig. 56: Repligator image for knit or crocheted fragments

Fig. 57: Complementary colour scheme generated in Repligator

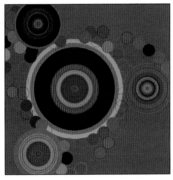

Fig. 58: Gliftic image – a design idea for crocheted circles

Fig. 59: A Gliftic idea for a crocheted garden wallhanging

Creating garment templates on the computer

There are several software packages on the market that will generate sewing patterns and/or knitting and crochet instructions, but the one I am most familiar with is Garment Designer by Cochenille Design Studio in California, which I will briefly describe.

I use Garment Designer for creating my freeform garment templates as it's so fast and easy. You can input your own measurements if you like or use any of the built-in standard sizes for women, men, children and babies. The program includes many design options, and you can add to these with Style Set 'plug-ins', as the developer creates new styles. The

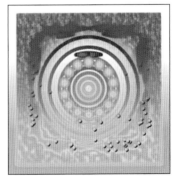

Fig. 60: An idea generated in Repligator for a colour gradation colour scheme

program also allows you to click and drag various points on a garment outline to create almost any shape you wish.

Once the pattern has been created, you print it onto A4 paper and join the sheets together with the aid of registration marks and numbered pages. Once the excess paper is trimmed away, the pattern is ready for use. See the 'Putting It All Together' chapter for more about using templates.

Fig. 61 is a screen shot of a garment created in Garment Designer. I used the Symmetry option to 'drag' the point of the left side down, making my garment 'asymmetrical' in design. Because I turned on the Front/Back Symmetry option, changes were made to the back pattern piece simultaneously, eliminating the possibility of error. If this option had been turned off, the changes to the jacket would have only occurred on the front left piece.

Fig. 61: Asymmetrical shawl collared jacket

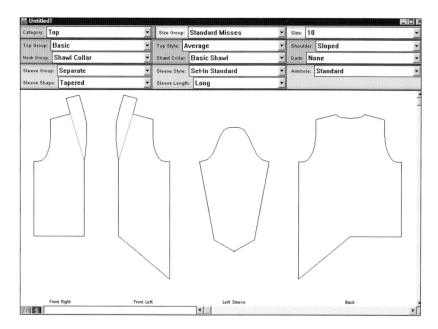

This design would look great with the body knitted, crocheted or sewn, with a scrumbled collar for contrast.

From this brief overview of just some of the software options available, you can see that the computer is a valuable tool in helping to achieve your creative aims. If, like me, you enjoy working with them, take some time to search the Internet or check out the cover CDs on computer magazines for other programs that may appeal to your sense of 'design play'.

Other pattern-making software programs include: Fittingly Sew, Dress Shop 4, Pattern Maker and Cameo/Pattern Master Boutique. See 'Resources' for information on where to obtain these programs.

Fragments –
An Introduction

'*Fragment*, n. 1. a part broken off or detached: scattered 2. a part that is incomplete 3. an odd piece, bit, or scrap'

The above definition of 'fragment' from *The Pocket Macquarie Dictionary* describes perfectly the scrumbled fragments used to create a unique wearable work of art. We join the fragments together, making the piece complete.

I cannot emphasise enough that the fragment patterns in this book are only meant to guide you through the process of scrumbling, i.e., to help beginners understand the 'concept' of scrumbling, and are not intended to be the only way of making them. Always following patterns stifles spontaneity and creativity.

The charm and excitement of this wonderful technique comes from the fact that you can throw the rules of traditional knitting and crochet out the window. For example, in freeform crochet, turning chains are not necessary because you don't have to worry about keeping the edges of your work straight or your rows parallel. And it doesn't matter if you join your yarn in the middle of a knit row with a knot! What is taboo in traditional knitting and crochet is actually encouraged in scrumbling. If you make a mistake, don't rip it out — turn it into a design element instead.

Once you have grasped the basic concept you will find your creativity taking over and in no time at all you will be creating your own fragments.

In the 'How to' chapter you will find a collection of crochet and knit stitches that you can use in your fragments, and in the 'FUNky FX' chapter there are lots of fun ideas.

In my own current crochet work, I generally let 'the yarn do the talking', instead of using lots of textured stitches, since I tend to work with lots of highly textured yarns. My favourite and most often used textured stitches are treble (US dc), bobbles, trailing stitch, corded rib stitch (also known as crab stitch), and limpets in small groups of three.

I very occasionally use a treble (US dc) circle (see 'How to' chapter) for covering small gaps that appear after stitching the fragments together or to add interest to an otherwise flat area of work.

When adding knitting to crocheted fragments I almost always use garter stitch or stocking stitch. This makes it easy to change the shape of a fragment that is perhaps becoming too linear by using short row or partial knitting (see 'How to' chapter).

If you wish to use home spun or plain yarns only, you may like to use more textured stitches; on the other hand, you may prefer to use the basic stitches and change direction often to give your work a free-flowing, abstract feel. You should do whatever feels right for you! Since there is no right or wrong way to scrumble you can choose whatever method you like to create your own style. Individuality of expression is what it's all about!

As mentioned previously, the appeal of scrumbling comes from the design freedom the technique offers. This means that it is not absolutely crucial that your end results look exactly the same as the fragment patterns illustrated in this book. In fact, it will be virtually impossible for them to do so if for no other reason than you will be using totally different yarns from those I used! Your interpretation of the instructions may also differ, and that is fine! I encourage you not to rip out stitches or worry if you don't end up with exactly the same number of stitches that I had. And if at any time while following my instructions you feel that you must add another bobble or use another textured stitch, then do so! Remember, too, that although the instructions call for at least six different yarns, those six may come from a total of 50 or more if you have that many in your selection to choose from.

Crochet hook sizes

I generally work with a size 5 mm (US 7) crochet hook as it tends to suit most of the yarns I use. Occasionally I change to a 5.5 mm (US 8) or 6 mm (US 9) if the yarn I want to use is particularly bulky, or down to a size 4.5 mm (US 6) if it's finer than an 8 ply (DK).

Knitting needle sizes

I use a variety of needle sizes depending on the effect I want and the thickness of the yarn. I also use two needles of different sizes because it adds a little extra texture to the fabric. A good range is 4.5 mm (US 7), 5 mm (US 8) and 6 mm (US 10½).

Note: The hook and needle sizes mentioned here are a guide only and you should use whatever you feel comfortable with.

Tip: If you cast off (bind off) with a smaller sized needle, the fabric will curve in slightly; if you cast off with a larger size, the fabric will curve outwards.

Crochet Fragments

'Closing our minds to ideas slams the door on all life's possibilities.'

UNKNOWN

I realise that following patterns for creating freeform fragments is contradictory to the freeform principle and may be a somewhat difficult idea for you to get your head around. However, if you think of the patterns as a means to an end, you will see that the end does, after all, justify the means.

All the stitches used are in the 'Crochet Stitch Collection'.

Crochet fragment 1

This first fragment has no textured stitches in it at all. Rather, I chose to use mostly textured yarns and let them do all the work for me. This is an option if you don't want to use textured stitches in your work, or you may prefer to use just one textured stitch as a feature, as I did in the 'Tracks' shawl (see 'Gallery'). 'Tracks' was created using the basic stitches plus corded rib stitch only.

Stitches used were dc (US sc), htr (US hdc), tr (US dc), dtr (US tr), tr tr (US dtr) and garter stitch.

YOU WILL NEED

An assortment of five yarns with varying textures in your chosen colour scheme

Crochet hook and knitting needles in the size of your choice

ABBREVIATIONS

ch	chain
st(s)	stitch(es)
dc(sc)	double crochet (single crochet)
htr(hdc)	half treble (half double crochet)
tr(dc)	treble (double crochet)
dtr(tr)	double treble (treble)
tr tr(dtr)	triple treble (double treble)

Fig. 62

INSTRUCTIONS

1st Row: Chain 10 then work 1 dc (US sc) in 2nd ch from hook, 1 htr (US hdc) in next 2 sts, 1 tr (US dc) in next 3 sts and 1dtr (US tr) in next 3 sts (9 sts). Turn.

Change yarn.

2nd Row: 5 tr (US dc) in first st, 1 htr (US hdc) in next 3 sts, 1 tr (US dc) in next 4 sts, 5 tr (US dc) in last st. Do not turn. You will now work along the original cast-on chain.

Transfer the stitch on your hook to a knitting needle, then pick up and knit 10 sts along the original cast-on edge (11 sts in all).

Rows 4–8: Knit.

Change yarn and knit two more rows. Cast off (bind off) all but the last stitch. Transfer this stitch to your crochet hook but do not turn.

Working down the side of the fragment make 3 ch, then work 6 tr (US dc) along the edge. Turn.

Change yarn, 3 ch, work 6 tr (US dc) to end, then 4 tr (US dc) in corner, 1 htr (US hdc) in next st, then dc (US sc) to end. Turn.

Change yarn, 1 ch, then work 1 dc (US sc), 1 tr (US dc), 1 dtr (US tr), 1 tr tr (US dtr), 2 dtr (US tr), 2 tr (US dc), 1 dc (US sc) along row. Fasten off.

Crochet fragment 2

Textured stitches used in this fragment were bent bobble, crab (or corded rib) and trailing stitch. (See 'Stitch Collection'.)

YOU WILL NEED

An assortment of five yarns of varying textures in your chosen colour scheme

A crochet hook and knitting needles in the size of your choice

ABBREVIATIONS

ch	chain
dc(sc)	double crochet (single crochet)
htr(hdc)	half treble (half double crochet)
tr(dc)	treble (double crochet)
dtr(tr)	double treble (treble)
RS	right side

Fig. 63

INSTRUCTIONS

1st Row: Chain 10.

2nd Row: 1 dc (US sc) into 2nd ch from hook, 2 htr (US hdc), 3 tr (US dc), 3 dtr (US tr) (9 sts). Turn.

3rd Row: 2 ch, 1 bent bobble in 2nd ch from hook, * 1 dc in next st, 1 bent bobble in next st*. Rep from * to * one more time, then dc (US sc) to end of row.

4th Row: *Change yarn.* 2 ch, then work 14 tr along top of previous bobble row (see tip below). *Do not turn.*

5th Row: Work corded rib st (crab st) back along the top of treble (US dc) row just worked making sure to work into the *front loop only* (this is important as you will see in the next row).

6th Row: *Change yarn.* Work a 'hill' into loops *behind* the row of corded rib as follows: 2 ch, 4 htr (US hdc), 5 tr, 4 dtr (US tr). Fasten off.

7th Row: With RS facing, flip fragment so that the original starting chain is at the top and RS is facing.

With knitting needles, pick up and knit 9 sts evenly along the original starting chain. *This counts as 1 row.* Knit 5 more rows. Right side of work should be facing you. Cast off, transferring last stitch to crochet hook. *Do not turn.*

14th Row: *Change yarn.* 2 ch, work a row of 9 htr (US hdc) along side of work to ridge of crab st. Turn.

15th Row: 2 ch, work a row of dc (US sc) to end. Turn.

16th Row: *Change yarn.* 2 ch, 1 tr in 2nd ch from hook, 1 tr (US dc) in next st, 1 Trailing St, 1 tr (US dc) in next two sts, 1 Trailing St, 1 tr (US dc) in each of last 4 sts. Break yarn and fasten off.

Tip: When working stitches on top of bobbles, work into the stitch just before the 1st bobble, then into a loop at the top of the bobble, then into the loop at the left-hand side of the bobble. Work one stitch between any two bobbles before proceeding as above to the end.

Crochet fragment 3

Textured stitches used in this fragment were bent bobble and corded rib.

YOU WILL NEED

An assortment of six yarns of varying textures in your chosen colour scheme

A crochet hook and knitting needles in the size of your choice

Fig. 64

ABBREVIATIONS

ch	chain
dc(sc)	double crochet (single crochet)
htr(hdc)	half treble (half double crochet)
tr(dc)	treble (double crochet)
dtr(tr)	double treble (treble)
RS	right side
cast off	bind off

INSTRUCTIONS

1st Row: 4 ch, join into a circle with a slip stitch.

2nd Row: Chain 3. Work 12 tr (US dc) into circle. Slip stitch to top of 3 ch.

3rd Row: *Change yarn.* 3 ch, 1 tr (US dc) into same place as 3 ch, 2 tr (US dc) into next st, 1 dtr (US tr) into next st. Turn.

4th Row: 2 ch, 1 bent bobble into next st, 1 dc (US sc) into next st, 1 bent bobble into next st, 1dc. Turn.

5th Row: *Change yarn.* 2 ch, then work 6 tr (US dc) along the top of the bobbles as described in Fragment 2 and 'How to' chapter of this book. Do not turn.

6th Row: Continuing in the same direction work 1 ch, then work the following sequence of stitches down the side of your work:

1 dc (US sc) into each of next 2 spaces

1 htr (US hdc) into each of next 2 spaces

1 tr (US dc) into next space, 2 tr (US dc) into next space (you have increased one stitch)

2 dtr (US tr) into next space (another increase)

2 tr (US dc) tr (US dc) into next space. Turn.

7th Row: *Change yarn.* Work 1 dc (US sc) into each of next 10 sts. Turn.

8th Row: Work 1 dc (US sc) into next stitch, and then:

1 htr (US hdc) into each of next 2 sts

1 tr (US dc) into each of next 2 sts

1 dtr (US tr) into each of next 3 sts.

Do not turn.

9th Row: *Change yarn.* Work corded rib stitch back along the row just worked, making sure to work into front loop only.

Do not turn. Transfer stitch to knitting needle.

10th Row: Pick up 9–10 stitches (one more or less won't really matter), using the loops behind the row of corded rib just worked.

Rows 11–14: Knit. Cast off.

Turn fragment so that the treble (US dc) circle is at the top, and with RS facing, join in new yarn to first free stitch at right-hand side of circle.

15th Row: With crochet hook, make 3 ch, then work 1 tr (US dc) into same place as 3 ch. Work 2 tr (US dc) into each stitch around circle. Slip stitch to top of first stitch behind bobble. *Do not turn.*

Transfer stitch to knitting needles.

16th Row: *Change yarn.* Pick up 12–13 sts.

Rows 17–22: Knit

23rd Row: Cast off.

Crochet fragment 4

Textured stitches used in this fragment were bent bobble and trailing stitch.

YOU WILL NEED

An assortment of five yarns with varying textures in your chosen colour scheme

A crochet hook and knitting needles in the size of your choice

ABBREVIATIONS

ch	chain
sts	stitches
K2 tog	knit two together
ss	slip stitch
dc(sc)	double crochet (single crochet)
htr(hdc)	half treble (half double crochet)
tr(dc)	treble (double crochet)
dtr(tr)	double treble (treble)
RS	right side

INSTRUCTIONS

1st Row: With size 4.5mm (US 7) knitting needles (or size of your choice) cast on 14 sts.

Knit 6 rows.

7th Row: *Change yarn*, K2 tog, knit to end.

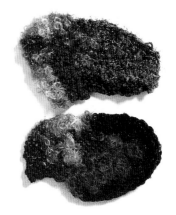

Fig. 65

8th Row: Knit to last 2 sts, K2 tog.

9th Row: K2 tog, knit to end.

10th Row: As 8th Row.

11th Row: As 9th Row.

12th Row: As 8th Row.

13th Row: Cast off, leaving last stitch and transfer to crochet hook. *Do not turn.*

14th Row: *Change yarn.* Continue along the left-hand side of fragment, working the following sts between the bumps formed by the garter stitch rows:

1dc in space (as close to hook as you can)

1 htr (US hdc) in next space

1 tr (US dc) in next space

2 tr (US dc) in next space

2 dtr (US tr) in next space

1 dtr (US tr) in next space.

Turn.

15th Row: 2 ch, then in 3rd ch from hook work 1 bent bobble, 1 dc (US sc), 1 bent bobble, 1 dc (US sc). Treble to end.

Turn.

16th Row: *Change yarn.* Work a 'hill' along the row and behind the bobbles as follows:

1dc in first st

1 htr (US hdc) in each of next 2 sts

1 tr (US dc) in each of next 2 sts.

Then continue in htr (US hdc) until you are just to the right of the first bobble worked in the previous row. Into the top of this bobble work:

1 tr (US dc), then

1 tr (US dc) into loop at side of bobble

1 dtr (US tr) in dc (US sc) between bobbles

1 dtr (US tr) into top of next bobble

1 dtr (US tr) into side of bobble.

Do not turn. Continue working in the same direction. Work 3 dtr (US tr) into same place as last dtr (US tr) was worked to make turning the corner easier.

Working along the side of previously crocheted rows, work:

3 dtr (US tr) into next space

3 tr (US dc) along stem of dtr (US tr) in row below.

Work 1 htr (US hdc), 1 dc (US sc) into next space and ss into next space to create a gentle end to the taper. Do not turn. Continue working in the same direction along the edge of the fragment.

Change yarn. Work the following:

> 1 trailing st using 3 or 4 wraps (see 'Stitch Collection'), picking up anchor loops from below knitted section
>
> dc (US sc) in each of the next 3 spaces
>
> 1 trailing st as before
>
> 1 dc (US sc) into next two spaces. Turn.

17th Row: Work a 'hill' as follows:

> 1 dc (US sc) in first stitch
>
> 1 htr (US hdc) in next st
>
> 1 tr (US dc) in each of next 2 sts
>
> 3 tr (US dc) in next st
>
> 1 htr (US hdc) in next, 1 dc (US sc) in next and ss in next st.

Break yarn and fasten off.

If you prefer, you can crochet fragments using plain yarns in dc (US sc), htr (US hdc) or treble (US dc) and surface crochet over the top of them later. Let your yarn and hook ramble at will and remember that an organic or amorphous shape is what you are after, not necessarily a geometric or linear shape, although if you want to work in a linear fashion then there is no rule to say you can't! Have a look at the pre-drawn template ideas in the following chapter — they would also make great crochet templates!

Knit Fragments

'*We keep moving forward, opening new doors, and doing new things, because we're curious and curiosity keeps leading us down new paths.*'

WALT DISNEY

As with the crocheted fragments, I have included patterns for two knitted fragments for you to practise on. Further on in this section I will talk about other ways of creating your own knit fragments.

You will need an assortment of yarns in your chosen colour scheme and a selection of needles in various sizes: say, 4 mm (US 6) and 6.5 mm (US 10½).

You may choose to use a pair of needles of the same size or one 4 mm (US 6) and one 6.5 mm (US 10½).

Work in garter stitch throughout and don't worry if the number of stitches you have at any given stage differs from mine. It really won't matter!

You may choose to leave long ends to use for surface crocheting at each yarn change, or you may introduce yarns of your choice after the fragment is complete.

Knit fragment 1

ABBREVIATIONS

K2 tog	knit two together
st(s)	stitch(es)
rem	remaining
inc	increase

INSTRUCTIONS

Cast on 10 sts.

Rows 1–5: Work 5 rows in garter stitch. Change yarn.

6th Row: K2 tog, knit 6 sts, K2 tog (8 sts rem).

7th Row: K2 tog, knit 4, K2 tog (6 sts rem).

8th Row: Knit 1, inc one st in next st, knit to end (7 sts rem).

Fig. 66

9th Row: Knit to last stitch and inc 1 st (8 sts).

10th Row: Knit.

11th Row: K2 tog. Knit to last stitch and inc 1 st.

12th Row: Cast on 3 sts (11 sts) and knit 2 rows. Change yarn.

15th Row: Knit 4 rows.

20th Row: Cast off, leaving last stitch on needle and pick up 8–9 stitches along side of work.

Row 21–24: Knit 4 rows. Change yarn.

Rows 25–28: Knit 4 rows. Change yarn.

Rows 29–36: Knit 8 rows. Cast off.

Knit fragment 2

ABBREVIATIONS

K2 tog	knit two together
st(s)	stitch(es)
rem	remaining
inc	increase

INSTRUCTIONS

Cast on 16 sts

1st Row: Knit.

2nd Row: Knit 2 tog, knit 12 sts, knit 2 tog.

3rd Row: Knit.

4th Row: Knit 2 tog, knit 10 sts, knit 2 tog.

5th Row: Knit 5 sts. Change yarn leaving long ends, knit to end.

6th Row: Knit 2 tog, knit to last 2 sts, knit 2 tog.

7th Row: Knit.

8th Row: Knit 2 tog, knit to last 2 sts, knit 2 tog.

Fig. 67

9th Row: As 7th row.

10th Row: As 8th row.

Rows 11–14: Repeat last 2 rows until 2 sts rem.

15th Row: Knit 2 tog, leaving last stitch on needle. Change yarn, then pick up 11 or 12 sts along side of work.

Rows 16–20: Knit 5 rows, increasing 1 st at beginning of each alternate row.

Rows 21–26: Change yarn and knit 6 rows.

27th Row: Cast off, leaving last stitch on needle. Change yarn, then pick up 7 sts along side of work (you should have 8 sts).

Rows 28–35: Knit 8 rows.

36th Row: Knit 3, knit 2 tog, knit 3 (7 sts).

37th Row: Knit 3, knit 2 tog, knit 2 (6).

38th Row: Knit 2, knit 2 tog, knit 2 (5).

39th Row: Cast off remaining 5 sts.

If you chose to use plain yarns and leave long ends, you can now use these to work surface crochet randomly over the surface of the fragments. Or you could embellish your fragments with freeform embroidery (couched threads, chain stitch, French knots), or add beads, buttons, tassels etc., or a combination of both surface crochet and embroidery. Or you could use knitted add-ons (see funky fx chapter).

A combination of the above two fragments was used to make the 'Red Sky at Night' bag, shown in Fig. 68 as a work in progress, to illustrate how the knit fragments are assembled working from the centre out.

Fig. 68

Creating your own knit fragments

Knit fragments are easier to construct than crocheted fragments since they are basically worked in garter stitch with random shaping. I don't use any stitch patterns at all, preferring to let the textures of the yarns I'm using do all the work or to add surface embellishment afterwards.

VERSION 1

Fig. 69 shows a sample of knitting in the 'any which way' method that illustrates how changing yarns and direction often creates interesting and unique fabrics without the need for complicated stitch patterns.

VERSION 2

While working with pre-drawn shapes isn't necessary, it can be fun to work that way. A new approach will 'grow' your creative repertoire and will certainly help that dreaded creative block we all experience from time to time.

Fig. 69

The shapes in Fig. 70 were created using Paint Shop Pro; however, you can freehand draw them if you prefer.

Figs 71 and 72 show a drawn shape and the resultant knitted fragment. You can see that artistic licence has been employed in that the knitted shape isn't an exact replica of the drawn one, nor does it have to be. Since we are working in a freeform manner it becomes almost mandatory that you view artistic licence as a creative tool and not be afraid to use it.

If you are worried about the short rows being visible in your knit fragments remember that they will be disguised by surface embellishment or be less noticeable when the fragments are knitted in fancy yarns (see Fig. 69 above).

Knitted fragments can be hand stitched together in the same manner as the crochet fragments (see 'Putting It All Together') or crocheted together. Surface crochet or embroidery can be added to disguise the seams if required. Meandering lines of surface chain along the seams can also make an effective contrast (see 'How to' chapter, 'Surface crochet method 1').

Of course, you don't need to create randomly shaped knit fragments. Fig. 73 shows surface embellishment of a garter stitch diamond shape. In the 'Log Cabin Knitting' section we look at using squares. Experiment!

Fig. 70

Fig. 71

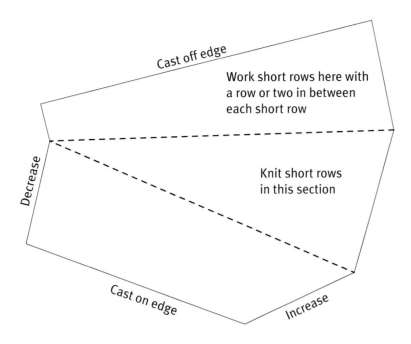

Cast off edge

Work short rows here with
a row or two in between
each short row

Decrease

Knit short rows
in this section

Cast on edge

Increase

Fig. 72

Fig. 73

Projects

Special contributions

I gratefully acknowledge the generosity of my very talented friends who contributed to the projects in the following chapter.

THE SCARF THAT GREW© 2003

THE ZEBRA BAG© 2003

Alison Vincent, Sydney, Australia

I first met Alison when she attended one of my scrumbling workshops a few years ago and she has become a steadfast and very supportive friend. Her creative talent has been an absolute joy to observe. She has an unerring ability to take what one teaches her and transform the knowledge into a style uniquely her own, something I as a tutor applaud! Alison's 'Scarf That Grew' makes its debut in this book.

NATIVE BLOSSOM HAT© 2002

FOLD'N ROLLED HAT© 2002

Lynne Johnson, Canberra, Australia

Lynne is an extremely talented knitter whose work I admire enormously and whose friendship I value highly. Her techniques fit perfectly into the 'taking your yarn for a walk' genre and I am thrilled that she chose to 'publish' her techniques for the first time in this book.

If you have the chance to take a workshop with Lynne, do so! They are great fun and she is a very knowledgeable woman, who does not hesitate to share her expertise! You can contact her at:

Tel: 02 6281 6771

Email: johnos@cyberone.com.au

Website: www.womenoffibre.com.au

METALLIC TUNIC WITH FLORAL APPLIQUÉ©
2002

Margaret Hubert, Pawling NY, USA

Margaret is proof of just how wonderful technology is and I wouldn't have met her if it hadn't been for the Internet! We share membership on a number of textile related email lists and it's through those lists that we got to know one another. I was lucky enough to meet her in person in October 2003 when she travelled to Australia to attend the 2003 Geelong Fibre Forum. Margaret is yet another very talented person who kindly let me use her 'Metallic Tunic' idea.

Margaret teaches freeform knitting and crochet in the US and in 2003 released her *Freeform Crochet and Freeform Knitting* videos. You can contact her by:

Email: MHDesigner@aol.com

Website: www.margarethubertoriginals.com

Crochet
Fragment Beret

To make this beret you will need a large dinner plate to use as a template. You can either work directly onto the plate (as I sometimes do, as I find the shape of the plate gives a nice rounded fullness to the joined fragments) or cut yourself a template from calico or cotton sheeting, using the plate as a guide.

This beret is based on Crochet Fragment 2. For my beret (see Fig. 74) I used nine full fragments and one half fragment, but this depends to a certain extent on the yarns used. Thicker yarns will of course make the fragments larger and vice versa with thinner yarns. You may also find that, once you start pinning your fragments to the template, it will be harder to 'fit' the fragments into the remaining spaces. If this is the case, choose some thinner yarns from your colour scheme for the final one or two fragments.

Place the fragments onto the template, moving them around until you are happy with the arrangement. Remember that it is unlikely that your fragments will completely fill the template shape and that perhaps a half fragment will be required to complete the circle.

If you are using a fabric template, once you are happy with the arrangement you can pin the fragments down with safety pins before you begin joining them. If you are working directly on the dinner plate, you can pin the fragments together at their edges to give some stability while you stitch, or you may choose to begin stitching without pinning. This technique is fine providing that you keep the plate under your work as a guide.

For your stitching yarn, choose a plain yarn from your colour scheme that is reasonably strong and that compliments the other yarns in the beret.

With right side facing, begin stitching the fragments together using a simple overhand stitch. The stitches won't be obvious in the finished beret because they will blend into the background fabric. I sew all my scrumbled garments together like this and no-one can ever tell me where each scrumble is joined!

If you find that small areas between the fragments don't quite join up, don't worry — this is easily fixed later. Leave them for now and

Fig. 74

continue somewhere else. Conversely, if you find two fragments are fighting for space, overlap them or hold the wrong sides together and join them with crochet. The resultant bump or ridge will just add to the texture of the fabric.

When all the fragments are joined, it's time to fill in any gaps around the edges and to deal with any small gaps in the centre. The best way to fix the edges is to pick up the fabric and fill in the spaces using simple stitches such as dc (US sc), htr (US hdc) and trebles (US dc).

The easiest way to cover gaps in the centre of the fabric is to stitch a small treble (US dc) circle to the top of the fabric. You may like to add one or two more of these somewhere else, whether required or not, to balance the overall design. In time you will discover your own easy solutions to any problems you may encounter in your work. This is yet another indication of the design freedom inherent to the scrumbling technique.

Note: Although it's not necessary to have a perfectly even edge, you should nevertheless keep an eye on the shape in order to avoid enlarging the original template shape too much.

Tip: For more information on how to assemble your fragments, see the 'Putting It All Together' chapter.

Adding the band

Now it's time to add the band that will make the beret fit your head. Once again, choose a plain yarn that compliments the overall colour scheme of your beret and a hook to match the yarn size. For example, for 8 ply (DK) you would probably use a 4 mm (US 5) or 4.5 mm (US 6) hook.

Work a row of dc (US sc) evenly around the edge of the fabric. When the round is complete slip stitch into the first dc (US sc). You may like to place a thread or a safety pin at this join to indicate the beginning and end of each round.

Continue working in rounds, decreasing evenly until the beret fits your head. I usually find that 10–12 rows are sufficient, but this of course depends a little on your head size and design preference. If you want to be more precise when decreasing, count the number of dc (US sc) in the first round and then divide it evenly. For example, if you have 120 dc (US sc), you might like to decrease every 10th stitch in the first decrease row and then every 9th, 8th, 7th, etc.

When you are happy with the size of the band, join the final round with a slip stitch, break off the yarn and sew in the ends.

Knit Fragment Bag

('Red Sky at Night' – see Fig. 68)

A combination of Knit Fragments 1 and 2 were used to make this bag. You can use these for your bag or create your own fragments.

You will need

A selection of yarns in your chosen colour scheme

Knitting needles, one of size 4mm (US 6), one of size 6.5mm (US 10½) and a pair of 3.5mm (US 4) (you will be knitting with different sized needles throughout)

Crochet hook, 4.5mm (US 6)

Template, 30cm (12") x 30cm (12")

Safety pins

Suitable fabric for lining

You will need approximately six to seven whole fragments, although this will depend somewhat on the yarns you use.

When you have at least six fragments made, start laying them out on the template until you are happy with the arrangement, making sure you have a good balance of colour and texture. It's a little like putting the pieces of a jigsaw puzzle together. You should find that the odd-shaped pieces do fit together reasonably well, with just a little coaxing required.

Tip: I find it easier to work from the centre of the template out, rather than the other way around.

If you find fragments want to overlap, let them do so, stitching one down on top of the other. Conversely, if you are left with small gaps, leave them for now. We'll get to those later. You will certainly have gaps around the edges, as these cannot be avoided.

When you have enough fragments to fill in the major part of the template and you have arranged the fragments to your satisfaction, pin them down with safety pins so that they won't move around too much as you stitch them together. It's easier to use a simple overstitch and sew them together from the right side, so choose a yarn that is compatible with the overall colour scheme of your bag. The yarn will blend in and be indistinguishable once all the fragments have been joined together. The act of stitching the fragments together, whether they be crocheted or knit fragments, will tend to *compact* your work slightly. This is normal and is addressed in the following paragraph.

Once you have the main area of your bag completed, it's time to start knitting smaller fragments to fill the outside gaps caused by the inevitable compaction mentioned above and by the fragments not fitting the template area exactly. These little fragment fillers are really easy to knit — it's just a matter of casting on a number of stitches, holding these near the gap you are filling to judge the correct number of stitches, and knitting a shape that roughly compares to each gap. You can, if you prefer, place a sheet of paper under each empty gap and draw the shape onto the paper to use as a mini template.

Tip: It's safer to have a stitch or two more than you think you will need, and a couple of extra rows won't hurt either. Then it's just a matter of knitting and shaping, all the while checking the fragments against the main bag until they 'fit' the gaps.

By now your template should be just about filled with knit fragments, and all that is left to do is perhaps fill one or two small gaps in the centre of your work where fragments haven't quite joined. You can either knit a very small piece or crochet a little treble (US dc) circle and stitch it over the gap.

Tiny uneven edges around the outside of the bag can be very quickly filled with a few dcs (US scs), as this is sometimes easier than picking up stitches and knitting a row. You will inevitably find your own solutions to filling in gaps and, once you've done it a couple of times, you will find that the process isn't as fiddly as it appears when just reading about it.

Finishing

To complete the bag, knit or crochet a plain back or make more fragments if you want a double-sided bag. Stitch the front and back together using mattress stitch and line the bag according to the instructions in the 'How to' chapter.

Strap

With 8 ply (DK) yarn in a colour that complements your bag, cast on 4 stitches with size 3.5mm (US 4) needles and knit in garter stitch until the work measures 115cm (45") or the length required. Make two more of these, and plait them together to make a really firm strap. Stitch down 5cm (2") of the strap to each side of the bag, making sure that it is stitched securely. Add a tassel or other embellishment to the end of each strap.

You can use a Caterpillar Braid or Crochet I-Cord (see 'FUNky FX' chapter) if you prefer.

If a closure is required, cast on 3 stitches and knit a 10cm (4") length of garter stitch for a loop. Fold in half and stitch securely to the centre of the back. Sew a button to the front of the bag.

A firmer, wider strap can be made by working dcs (US scs) over 12–15 chain in 8 ply (DK) with a smaller hook than is generally recommended.

Log Cabin Knitted Bag

This fun and easy technique, inspired by a picture of a log cabin quilt, is a follow-on from the knitted fragment idea where the shapes were knitted and then embellished with embroidery stiches, such as chain stitch, French knots, couching and cross stitch. In fact, any of your favourite stitches can be used, as well as surface crochet and/or knitted 'bits'. (See the 'FUNky FX' chapter for some ideas.)

Garter stitch was used throughout this item. No gauge is required.

As with all the freeform 'patterns' in this book, you don't need to worry if the number of stitches you find on your needles is the same as the number of stitches in the instructions, as long as the variance isn't great. One or two stitches more or less is perfectly acceptable.

Note: It's important that you cast off loosely when you have completed your log cabin segments. You may choose to leave long ends at each yarn change that you can then use for embellishing the surface or you may prefer to introduce new yarns once the piece has been knitted.

Log cabin crochet follows the same principles as the knitted version except that you just tie in a new yarn at the beginning of each new segment.

You will need

A colour scheme of 12–15 yarns in a variety of textures and thicknesses

Knitting needles, 5mm (US 8)

Crochet hook, 5mm (US 7)

ABBREVIATIONS

st(s)   stitch(es)

dc(sc)   double crochet (single crochet)

Fig 75

Instructions

Cast on 10 sts, knit 5 rows. Cast off, leaving last stitch on needle.

Change yarn, turn work a quarter turn to the right and pick up 3 sts along side of work. (Pick up between the 'bumps' only). You will have 4 sts in total (this includes the last stitch from the cast off row). Knit 5 rows.

Cast off, leaving last stitch on needle, change yarn, and turn work a quarter turn to the right, pick up 13 sts (you should have a total of 14) and knit 5 rows.

Cast off, leaving last stitch on needle, change yarn, and turn work a quarter turn to the right, pick up 7 sts (8) and knit 5 rows.

Fig 75a: Diagonally knitted stripes

Fig 75b: Horizontal stripes

Cast off, leaving last stitch on needle, change yarn, and turn work a quarter turn to the right, pick up a stitch from each of the 'bumps' as before and knit 5 rows.

Continue in this manner until your square is the size required.

The bag in Fig. 75 measures 28cm (11") x 28cm (11") give or take a millimetre or two. If distortion has occurred at the edges, you can work some dc (US sc) along the edge to even things out.

If you prefer, you can knit a plain or striped background as your base fabric. The end result would still be very effective.

Finishing

To complete the back of the bag, you can work another square using the same technique as the front or knit one in garter stitch (using a slightly smaller gauge needle to create a firmer fabric) or crochet one in one of the basic stitches. If you use garter stitch, you can knit a tension swatch or use the template as a guide for your stitches and rows.

Using mattress stitch, stitch the sides and one edge together. Line bag according to the basic instructions in the 'How to' chapter.

Strap

You can knit or crochet a strap (see the 'How to' chapter for instructions).

Knitted Fragmented Strips Bag

Working in strips is a wonderful technique for using up scrap yarns or for indulging yourself in the joy of using an expensive yarn in the knowledge that it won't cost you a fortune. It is also one of my favourite ways of creating unique accessories, cushions and garments and a perfect way to 'take your yarn for a walk'.

Because you will be using so many different yarns of different plies and textures, it is impossible to determine a correct gauge. Therefore, as with the scrumbling technique, you will be able to let your creativity flow, unhindered by the traditional rules. Instead of working small fragments that are later joined, with the strip technique you knit or crochet lengths of fabric of whatever length and width you please.

Tip: Because you are using yarns of different weights and thicknesses you may need to occasionally double any thinner yarns in order to avoid major distortion at the edges of your strips.

Here are some suggestions for knitting and crocheting fragmented strips:

- Vary the number of stitches used for each strip.
- Vary the number of rows worked, or work exactly the same for each strip. Again, depending on the yarns used, each strip will be a different length. You can use this to your advantage in a garment to create an interesting, asymmetrical hemline.
- Use a combination of knitted strips and crocheted strips.
- Vary the hook and/or needle size as you knit the strips. For bags it is advisable to use a slightly smaller needle than normal to achieve a tighter fabric.
- Use two different sized needles when working the knitted strips. This has a tendency to create its own texture.
- Use garter stitch throughout or be adventurous and add your favourite stitch patterns. There are literally hundreds of stitch patterns available in as many books. Be aware, though, that a stitch pattern won't be shown to full advantage if worked in a heavily textured yarn.

Fig. 76

To get you started here are instructions for a small knitted bag that takes no time at all to knit, yet looks a million dollars when finished.

The finished bag measures approximately 19cm (7½") x 19cm (7½"). If you want a larger bag, simply add more stitches to the instructions as given — just a few more per strip will make the bag a few centimetres larger. Or, if you want a much larger size, make extra strips.

Garter stitch was used throughout this bag, plus selected FUNky FX was used randomly (see 'FUNky FX' chapter). No tension gauge is required for this project.

You will need

A selection of specialty yarns in your chosen colour combination, plus some plain coordinating yarn that will add contrast and achieve unity. (Use any finer yarns doubled or even trebled to avoid significant differences in strip widths. I call this 'edge creep'!)

Knitting needles, 5.5mm (US 9) (suggestion only) — since you will be using many different yarns it's difficult to ascertain which size needles should be used; as a general rule of thumb, when making fabric for bags or cushions use a size smaller than that indicated on the wrapper of your heavier yarns)

Crochet hook, 4.5mm (US 6)

Knitting needle, one of size 6.5mm (US 10½) for casting off

Lining of your choice

Button or bead

ABBREVIATIONS

st(s)	stitch(es)
K1	knit one
yfwd/wyif	yarn forward/with yarn in front
K2 tog	knit two together
yo	yarn over
rep	repeat

Instructions — first strip

You can use any configuration you wish, of course, but remember that the flap will hide a section of the strips so take that into consideration when deciding which end will be the flap end.

STRIPE 1

Cast on 10 sts with any yarn and knit 4–6 rows. The thicker the yarn, the fewer rows you will need. If a yarn is extremely chunky and brightly coloured, you may prefer to knit only 2 rows with it.

STRIPE 2

Change yarn and knit 4–6 rows. (The number of rows you choose to knit for each strip is up to you. I seldom knit more than 6 rows).

STRIPE 3

Change yarn and knit 5 stitches, turn and knit a further 4 rows on this first group of stitches. Break yarn. Place these 5 stitches onto a holder.

Join in yarn to the 2nd group of 5 stitches, knit 4 rows and break off yarn.

Fig. 77: Schematic
diagram showing how bag
was constructed

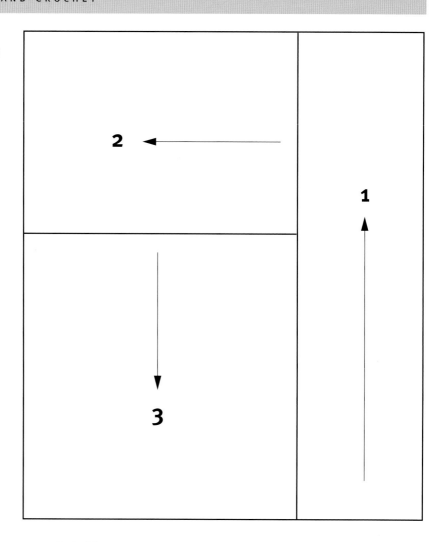

Transfer held stitches back to working needle.

Join in yarn to beginning of row and knit across both groups of stitches, securing loose thread to the working yarn as you knit across the slit.

STRIPE 4
Change yarn and knit 4 rows.

STRIPE 5
Make a row of eyelets as follows:

K1, * yfwd, K2 tog.* Repeat from * to * to end.

Knit 1 row.

STRIPE 6
Choose a yarn that is not too bulky (a smooth ribbon works well) and continue as follows in elongated stitch:

Knit 1 row.

Next row: K1, * yo twice, K1.* Rep from * to * until last stitch. K1.

Next row: Knit to end, dropping extra loops as you go.

Knit 3 rows and change yarn.

Continue knitting in stripes as above, interspersing plain knitted rows with any FUNky FX you like.

When your work measures 43cm (17"), cast off loosely using the size 6.5mm (US 10½) needle. Using a slightly larger needle will ensure that the cast-off edge remains loose.

Instructions — second strip

With right side of first strip facing, turn the work and pick up and knit 14 stitches (you can either pick up each 'bump' from the end of the previously worked garter stitch rows in the first strip, or between each 'bump', but not from both). From the schematic diagram in Fig. 77 you can see by the direction of the arrows just where I picked up for my 2nd and 3rd strips.

STRIPE 1
Knit 2–4 rows.

STRIPE 2
Change yarn and knit an eyelet row as in first strip (stripe 5).

STRIPE 3
Change yarn and knit a row of elongated stitch as in first strip (stripe 6), then knit 2 more rows of garter stitch.

STRIPES 4–7
Knit 4 more stripes of garter stitch, changing yarn for each one.

Measure the width of your bag. It should be approximately 19cm (7½"). If it's a little wider, that's fine — don't worry about it. If it's narrower than you would like it to be, work another stripe.

Instructions — third strip

Turn your work again and this time pick up stitches from the side of the strip just completed. I needed to pick up 16 stitches to ensure that I filled in the space created by knitting the second strip onto the side of the first strip. You may need to pick up more or less, depending on the yarns you have used.

Continue knitting stripes as before for the length of the bag — 43cm (17") in total.

Finishing

Fold the bag at 38cm (15") and sew sides using mattress stitch, leaving a 5cm (2") flap.

Lining

Tip: Remember to pre-shrink any lining fabric that may have a tendency to shrink when washed.

Since this is a freeform bag and you will certainly have used different yarns from those I used, it is likely that your bag won't measure exactly the same as mine. The general procedure for determining the size of the lining is as follows:

- Measure the total length of the bag *less the length of the flap*, and then add 4cm (1½") for the hem.

- Measure the width of the bag and add 4cm (1½") for a seam allowance.

Fold lining in half and sew the sides together. Without turning inside out, insert the lining into the bag. Fold under the top 2cm (¾") of the lining and slip stitch to the top of the bag, just below the edge.

Note: I didn't line the flaps of my bags, but if you choose to do so, you will need to cut out a pattern to include this extra length and stitch the lining down accordingly.

Flap

Finish off the flap as follows:

1st Row: Measure in approx. 2cm (¾") from edge of flap and with yarn of your choice pick up stitches evenly across work until you get to within 2cm (¾") from other edge.

2nd Row: Knit.

3rd Row: K2 tog, knit to last 2 sts, K2 tog.

4th Row: *Change yarn* and repeat 2nd row.

5th Row: Same as 2nd row.

Continue in this manner until the flap extension measures 3.5cm (1⅜")

6th Row: Cast off.

Work 1 row of dc (US sc) along side of flap. When you reach the cast off edge at the top of the flap make a chain loop across the top for a button closure, then continue along the other side of the flap.

Work 1 row of dc (US sc) along top edge of bag and fasten off. Sew on button.

Strap

Make a strap measuring 115cm (45") using two ends of yarn as per the instructions for Caterpillar Braid in the 'FUNky FX' chapter and attach securely to the sides of the bag.

Note: This bag is designed to be worn across the chest rather than over the shoulder.

Crocheted Fragmented Strips Bag

The finished bag measures approximately 19cm (7½") wide by 21cm (8¼") high, with an 8cm (3⅛") flap. If you want a larger bag, simply add more stitches to the instructions as given – just a few more per strip will make the bag a few centimetres larger. Or, if you want a much larger size, make extra strips.

The crocheted strips for this bag were worked using mainly dc (US sc) and half treble (US hdc) or trebles (US dc), together with highly textured yarns and some FUNky FX to add interest.

Refer to the suggestions for the previous knit version of this bag for ideas on how to make fragmented strips.

You will need

A selection of specialty yarns in your chosen colour combination, plus some plain coordinating yarn that will add contrast and achieve unity. (Use any finer yarns doubled or even trebled to avoid significant differences in strip width.)

Crochet hooks, 4.5mm (US 6) and 5mm (US 7). The larger hook should be used for any bulky yarns. When making fabric for a bag, use a smaller sized hook than usual to ensure a firmer fabric.

Lining of your choice

Button or bead

Fig 78

ABBREVIATIONS

ch	chain
dc(sc)	double crochet (single crochet)
dtr(tr)	double treble (treble)
htr(hdc)	half treble (half double crochet)
tr(dc)	treble (double crochet)
tr tr (dtr)	triple treble (double treble)
st(s)	stitch(es)
RS	right side

Fig 79: Diagram showing
how bag was constructed

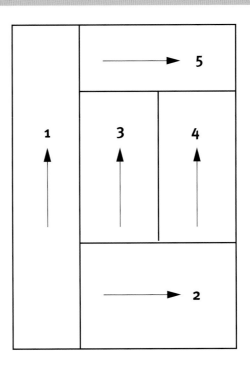

Instructions — first strip

The crocheted version of this bag was constructed using the following diagram. You may of course change any of the components to suit your own design.

Note: Turning chains aren't always necessary when working in a freeform manner. At the beginning of each row, work 1 chain (not counted as a stitch), and then work into each loop of the previously worked row. Initially, it may help to keep count as you work until you determine that you are keeping a constant number of stitches in your work.

Stripes 1 & 2: Ch 10, miss (US skip) 1 ch and work 2 rows of htr (US hdc) (9 sts).

Stripe 3: Work 1 row of trebles (US dc), turn. Work 4 dc (US sc), ch 3, miss (skip) 3sts, dc (US sc) to end. This makes a horizontal slit.

Stripe 4: 1 row of dc (US sc), 1 row of loop stitch, and then 1 row of dc (US sc).

Stripe 5: 2 rows of trebles (US dc).

Stripe 6: Work 3 dc (US sc), 1 trailing stitch, 2 dc (US sc), 1trailing stitch, 2 dc (US sc).

Stripe 7: 1 row of dc (US sc), 1 row of crumpled stitch — instead of using double treble (US tr) you can use tr tr (triple treble) (US dtr) for a more textured effect. This is sometimes necessary when using finer yarns. Then 1 row of dc (US sc).

Stripe 8: 2 rows of trebles (US dc).

Stripe 9: 1 row dc (US sc), 1 row wrapped bobble and 1 row dc (US sc).

Stripe 10: 1 row tr (US dc), 1 row dc (US sc) with horizontal slit, 1 row tr (US dc).

Stripe 11: 1 row dtr (US tr), 1 row dc (US sc).

Stripe 12: 2 rows htr (US hdc).

Stripe 13: 1 row tr (US dc) if using a heavily textured yarn, otherwise work 2 rows of tr (US dc).

Stripe 14: 1 row dc (US sc). *Do not turn*. Work 1 row of corded rib stitch into *front loop only* of previous row.

Stripe 15: 1 row tr (US dc) into back loops left in previous row, 1 row tr (US dc). Strip 16: 1 row long loop stitch, 1 row dc (US sc).

Stripe 17: 2 rows tr (US dc).

Instructions — second strip

To make the second strip, turn the first strip sideways, and with RS of work facing, work a row of treble (US dc) along 20 st (or number required to measure 15cm [6"]). Continue working stripes as before, using plain stitches together with an occasional row of a FUNky FX stitch until the work measures 9cm (3½") or width desired.

Instructions — third strip

The third strip is added by working across 7 stitches starting at the junction of where the first strip meets the second strip (approximately 6cm [2⅜"] in width). Work stripes as before.

Instructions — fourth strip

The fourth strip is added by working across the remainder of the stitches at the side of the first strip. Work stripes as before.

Before adding the fifth strip, you will need to stitch the third strip to the first strip and the fourth strip to the third strip.

Instructions — fifth strip

Now work the fifth strip by working across the top of the already joined third and fourth strips. Continue in stripes as before until this final section is the same length as the first strip. Stitch strip 5 to strip 1 and finish off according to the following instructions.

Lining

Tip: Remember to pre-shrink any lining fabric that may have a tendency to shrink when washed.

Since this is a freeform bag and you will certainly have used different yarns from those I used, it's likely that your bag won't measure exactly the same as mine.

The general procedure for determining the size of the lining is as follows:

• Measure the total length of the bag less the length of the flap, and then add 4cm (1½") for the hem.

• Measure the width of the bag and add 4cm (1½") for the seam allowance.

Fold bag at 29cm (11¼"), leaving 8cm (3") for a flap. Sew sides together.

Fold lining in half and sew sides together. Without turning bag inside out, insert the lining into the bag. Fold under the top 2cm (¾") of the lining and slip stitch to the top of the bag, just below the edge.

Note: I didn't line the flaps of my bags, but if you choose to do so you will need to cut out a pattern to include this extra length and stitch the lining down accordingly.

Flap

Mark the centre of the flap with a pin. With a yarn of your choice, work in dc (US sc) until within 1.5cm (½") of centre. Work a chain loop to measure 3cm (1¼") from 1.5cm (½") past the centre, insert hook into the fabric and continue working dc (US sc) to the end. Sew on button.

Strap

Make a strap measuring 115cm (45") using two ends of yarn as per the instructions for Caterpillar Braid in the 'FUNky FX' chapter and attach securely to the sides of the bag.

Note: This bag is designed to be worn across the chest rather than over the shoulder.

Scarf d'Opulence

W hile I have stipulated the yarns to be used for this project, it is by no means necessary to use the same ones in your scarf. The theory behind most of the projects in this book is that you, as the designer, may use whatever yarns you wish to complete a project.

The simple stitches (garter and elongated) used in this scarf enable you to easily adjust the length and/or width. No tension gauge is required for this project.

You will need

50 g (1¾ oz) ribbon yarn (I used Katia by Cleckheaton)

50 g (1¾ oz) Cleckheaton Faux Fur

50 g (1¾ oz) Fingering Metallic Mix, approx. 3 or 4 ply (Faux Fur and Metallic Mix are used together and referred to in the instructions as 'combo yarn')

Knitting needles, one each of 15mm (US 19) and 10mm (US 15) (you will be using one of each size needle throughout). *Note*: Using the larger needle for the cast on will ensure a looser edge, or you can use the thumb cast-on method (see 'How to' chapter)

Tip: Ribbon yarn has a tendency to twist during knitting. For this scarf, it is easier to ignore than to fix, as once the loops have been released and tugged gently downwards, it straightens itself out quite satisfactorily.

ABBREVIATIONS

st(s)	stitch(es)
yo	yarn over
K1	knit one

Instructions

With combo yarn and size 15mm (US 19) needle cast on 20 sts.

Knit 3 rows. Break off combo yarn leaving a 12 cm (4¾") tail. Join in ribbon yarn leaving a 12cm (4¾") tail and proceed as follows, making sure that each yo row is worked using the ribbon yarn (and the size

Fig. 80

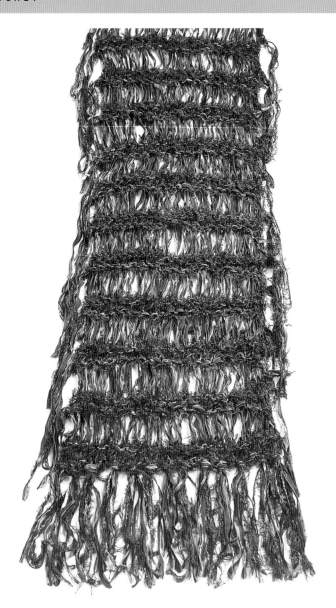

10mm [US 15] needle) and the three knit rows are worked using the combo yarn.

1st Row: K1, * yo twice, K1. Repeat from * across row.

2nd Row: Knit across row, dropping the extra loops.

3rd Row: Knit.

4th Row: Knit.

Continue in pattern until work measures length required, ending with 3 knit rows. Cast off using a 15mm (US 19) needle to ensure a looser cast off.

Note: Because the nature of this scarf makes it difficult to hide the ends from each yarn change I have chosen to turn them into a design element by leaving them to hang loose along the edges.

Fringe

Alternate 24cm (9½") lengths of combo yarn and ribbon yarn across the ends of the scarf. Attach by folding the lengths in half and pulling the folded edge through the fabric and feeding the two ends through this loop. Pull firmly to tighten. (See 'How to' chapter.)

Easy Crochet (or Knit) T-Square Shawl

The 'Homage to a Magpie' shawl (see 'Gallery') was created by crocheting individual fragments and linking them together with chains to form the triangular shape. Using a simple background as a base and embellishing it as you go or after you finish the fabric is the easiest method.

Stitch used may be either half trebles (half double crochet) or trebles (double crochet). No tension gauge is required for this project.

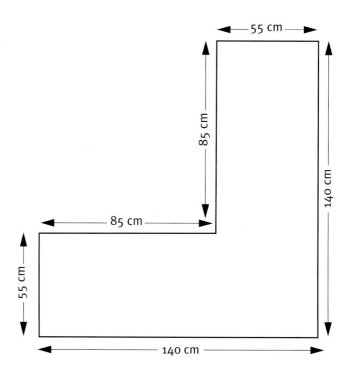

Fig. 81

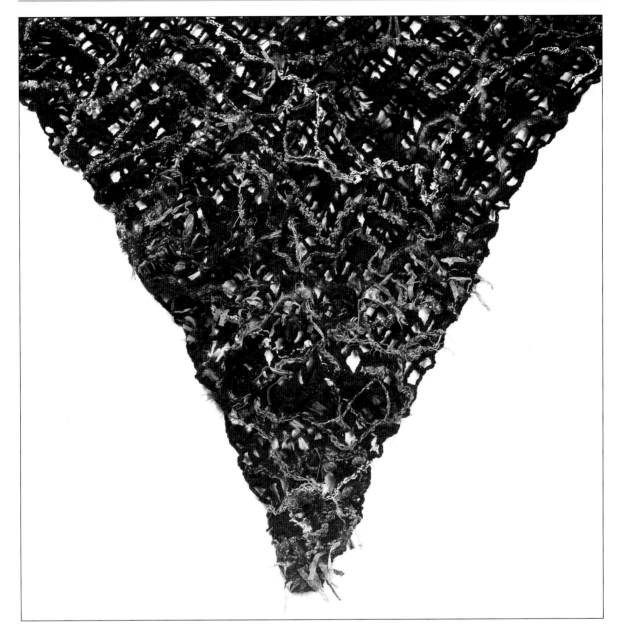

Fig. 82

You will need

200–250 g (7–9 oz) of yarn (wool, wool blend or mohair)

Crochet hook, 5mm (US 7)

Instructions

Chain enough stitches to measure 140cm (55"). If, after you have worked a few rows, it measures a little more, it won't really matter.
Work htr (US hdc) or treble (US dc) until work measures 55cm (21½").

With right side of work facing continue in your chosen stitch until the section measures 55cm (21½"). Turn and work on these stitches only until the long side of your work measures 140cm (55"). Fasten off.

Embellish with surface crochet as in Meandering Shawl (Fig. 82) or with one of the variations listed below.

Finally, add fringing (see 'How to' chapter).

Variations for shawl

- For an extravagant, unrestrained and joyful shawl use the luxury fringing technique from the 'FUNky FX' chapter as you build the base fabric.

- Instead of crocheting the shawl, use Lynne Johnson's Shaggy Reverse Stocking Stitch technique (see 'FUNky FX' chapter), which will give you a similar fabric.

- Scatter the surface with motifs from the 'FUNky FX' chapter or from your own collection of favourites.

- Instead of making a solid fabric for the base, use a mesh-type fabric.

The potential is unlimited! Experiment!

Chain Loop Beret

This design shows that a plain beret can be transformed into something special through the use of an unusual stitch as embellishment. It will fit an average head size.

What you need

100 g (3½oz) of 8 ply (DK)

1 ball contrast yarn (use a fancy yarn with texture for the best effect)

Crochet hook, 4mm (US 5)

ABBREVIATIONS

ch	chain
Rd	round
st(s)	stitch(es)
ss	slip stitch
tr(dc)	treble (double crochet)

Instructions

Note: The 3 ch at beg of each round count as 1st stitch.

To start: Make 4 ch, ss to 1st ch to form circle.

1st Rd: 3 ch, 11 tr (US dc) into circle (12 sts), ss to the top of 1st tr (US dc).

2nd Rd: 3 ch, 1 tr (US dc) in 1st, 2 tr (US dc) in each tr (US dc) to end (24 sts), ss to top of 1st tr (US dc).

3rd Rd: 3 ch, inc 1 tr (US dc) in every 2nd tr (US dc) (36 sts), ss to top of 1st tr (US dc).

4th Rd: 3 ch, inc 1 tr (US dc) in every 3rd tr (US dc) (48 sts), ss to top of 1st tr (US dc) (work should measure approx. 10cm (4") in diameter)

Rep the 4th round 7 times increasing one stitch in the 4th, 5th, 6th, 7th, 8th, 9th and 10th sts respectively (132 sts and 11 rounds).

12th Rd: 3 ch, evenly dec 12 tr (US dc) (see formula below), ss to top of 1st tr (US dc).

Fig. 83

Formula for decreasing 12 sts evenly in each round:

12th Rd: Work 10 tr, tr2 tog 12 times.

13th Rd: Work 9 tr, tr2 tog 12 times.

14th Rd: Work 8 tr, tr2 tog 12 times.

15th Rd: Work 7 tr, 2tr tog 12 times.

Repeat 12th Rd 3 more times (84 sts and 15 rounds).

Work 3 rounds of dc (US sc) and fasten off.

Embellishment

With the right side of the beret facing you, pick up a loop from the top of each of the treble (US dc) in the 1st, 3rd, 5th, 7th, 9th and 11th rounds and work a round of chain loops (see 'FUNky FX' chapter), one round at a time. Sew in ends.

Other hat ideas

- Knit or crochet a plain beret or cloche and add embellishment to the surface using crochet, knitted add-ons, embroidery, etc.
- Make a crown of four identical segments and crochet a band or brim.

Basic
Crocheted Bag

This basic bag can be made with or without the circular base and pockets. Fig. 84 shows the components of the bag and Fig. 85 shows the bag made without the base or pockets and embellished with an appliquéd decorative chain (see 'Funky FX' chapter). Fig. 86 shows the bag made with the base (no pockets) and embellished with floral motifs. Or you can make the bag with pockets and embellish them, instead of the bag itself, with ideas from the 'FUNky FX' chapter.

Half Treble (US hdc) was used throughout. **Note**: Correct tension isn't a requirement for this project!

Tip: For a knitted version of this bag you would need to make a swatch in your preferred stitch and calculate the stitches and rows required using the measurements shown below.

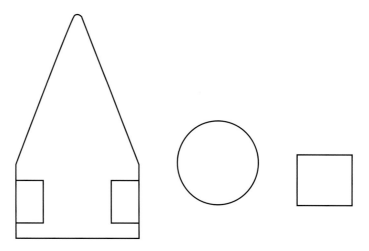

Fig. 84: Basic Bag components

Bag measurements

Fig. 85 (right) and
Fig. 86 (left)

Width of bag — 30cm (12")

Length to where shaping for handle starts— 17cm (6¾")

Length of handle — 34cm (13½")

Pockets — approx. 12cm (4¾") x 13.5cm (5¼") (placed evenly on the side
    seams approx. 3.8cm (1½") from bottom of bag)

Circular base (optional) — approx. 19cm (7½") in diameter

You will need

200 g (7 oz) of 8 ply (DK) yarn

Small amounts of specialty or contrasting yarns for embellishing (beads and/or buttons may also be used if desired)

Crochet hook, 4.5mm (US 6)

Lining if required

ABBREVIATIONS

ch	chain
htr(hdc)	half treble (half double treble)
inc 1 htr (US hdc)	2 htr (US hdc) in next stitch
htr2tog (hdc2tog	decrease is worked as follows: work the first stitch as an unfinished double crochet (US single crochet) and the second stitch as an unfinished half treble (US half double crochet), then pull the yarn through four loops to complete

Instructions

Special note: Begin each row with 1 ch as a turning chain and work the first stitch of each row directly into the stitch nearest the hook. The 1 ch does not count as a stitch and is used only to facilitate turning.

FRONT

Chain 46.

1st Row: Beginning in 3rd ch from hook work a row of htr (US hdc), 1 ch, turn.

2rd Row: Work htr (US hdc) to end, 1 ch, turn.

Repeat 2rd row until work measures 17cm (6¾") or depth required for the body of the bag (approx. 23 rows altogether).

SHAPING HANDLES

1st Row: htr2tog (US hdc2tog), htr (hdc) to last 2 sts, htr2tog (US hdc2tog), 1 ch, turn.

2nd Row: Work htr (US hdc) to end, 1 ch, turn.

Repeat rows 1 and 2 until 4 stitches remain.

Fasten off.

BACK

Repeat as for front.

BASE (OPTIONAL)

Chain 16.

1st Row: From 3rd chain from hook, work 14 htr (US hdc), 1ch, turn.

2nd Row: Inc 1htr (US hdc) twice (i.e., work 2htr (US hdc) in each of first 2 sts (you are increasing 2 sts at each end of row), htr (US hdc) to last 2 sts, inc 1htr (US hdc) twice, 1ch, turn (18 sts).

3rd Row: Inc 1 htr (US hdc), htr (US hdc) to last st, inc 1 htr (US hdc), 1ch, turn (20 sts).

4th Row: As 2rd row (24 sts).

5th Row: As 3rd row (26 sts).

6th Row: As 3rd Row (28 sts).

Work 10 rows of htr (US hdc) without shaping.

17th Row: htr2tog (US hdc2tog), htr (US hdc) to last 2 sts, htr2tog (US hdc2tog), 1ch, turn (26 sts).

18th Row: As 17th row (24 sts).

19th Row: (htr2tog/US hdc2tog) twice, htr (US hdc) to last 4 sts, (htr2tog/US hdc2tog) twice, 1 ch, turn (20 sts).

20th Row: As 17th row (18 sts).

21st Row: As 19th row (14 sts).

22nd Row: Work htr (US hdc) to end.

Fasten off.

POCKETS (OPTIONAL)

Chain 22.

1st Row: From 3rd chain from hook, work 20 htr (US hdc), 1ch, turn.

2nd Row: Work htr (US hdc) to end, 1ch, turn.

Repeat 2nd row until pocket measures approx. 12cm (5¼").

Fasten off.

Finishing

Complete all embellishments and stitch on all motifs before attaching the lining.

The handles of the bag may be lined if you wish; however, it's easier to line the bottom section only.

Cut a lining for all pieces as required, adding 1.5cm (½") all round for seams and hem. Sew seams, insert lining into bag, fold hem and slip stitch the lining to the fabric just below the point where the shaping begins.

Crocheted Wire Amulet Bag

To create a perfect freeform piece negates the very spirit of freeform!

JENNY DOWDE

For some time artists have been using wire to create wearable art. While most of them make jewellery pieces, it's also possible to create articles that can be worn as garments, provided a soft and flexible wire is used (see 'Bibliography' for titles on this subject).

To start you off on this new 'textile' adventure, I have included a pattern for a simple crocheted wire and bead amulet.

Once you get a feel for working with wire, you'll find that creating freeform pieces is easy!

Using wire instead of yarn does create some problems that you need to find solutions to, the main one being that wire has no stretch factor, unlike yarn, so that has to be taken into consideration when creating a piece that needs to fit, whether it be around your neck, your arm or your body. You may therefore prefer to make a swatch and work to a gauge. However, you can also freeform with wire, developing your design as you go.

The 'Memories' neckpiece (Fig. 87) was created in this way, beginning with a small circle of 4 chains. I then worked round and round until I reached the size I wanted. The circle isn't perfectly round, and wasn't ever intended to be so.

I started 'Crossing Circles' (Fig. 88) by crocheting around a rubber 'O' ring and then worked in rounds until I felt that it was big enough. I then worked around just over half the outside of the circle, stopped the round and continued straight up for the strap and back again, securing it to the other side.

'Verdigris' (Fig. 89) evolved as I worked. I had no preconceived idea when I started it and initially I didn't much like it. However, after leaving it aside for some weeks, I picked it up one day and started bending and twisting — basically just playing with it. To disguise a fold of 'fabric' I stitched the 3D circle over the top, added the strap and suddenly it looked OK!

In the 'Gallery' you will find more examples of wire work.

The hooks or needles you choose to use for your wire work are up to

Fig. 87

Fig. 88

you. In her book, *Knitting with Wire*, Nancie Wiseman advocates using wooden or bamboo needles, as the wire tends to slip over these far more easily. As I don't have any wooden needles, or hooks for that matter, I use metal ones. So far I've not encountered any problems.

Choosing the right wire

There are several wires available that you can choose from (see 'Resources' for more information).

ARTISTIC AND CRAFT WIRES

Artistic wire comes in a range of gauges and colours; craft wire is available in gold (more like brass), silver, black, red and green.

For most knitting and crochet projects I recommend that you choose a gauge between 28 and 34 as any heavier would be torture to use. You can use 26 gauge, but it's hard on your hands and takes longer to work.

Fig 89

Note: 'Cascade' (see 'Gallery') was made using gold (brass) craft wire and it did leave some black residue on my fingers as I worked, which I thought might be a problem down the track. Fortunately, it hasn't proven to be so. It doesn't leave marks on clothing and it's actually mellowed over a few years to a lovely 'antique' looking piece.

COPPER WINDING WIRE

This wire is my favourite, but it only comes in one colour. To overcome this, it is fun to use a coloured sewing thread with it to create colour shifts. I also like the fact that I can use this wire doubled to construct a slightly heavier 'fabric'.

It is available in several diameters (not gauges) and my preference is 0.2 mm (approximately 34 gauge). Anything higher than 0.3 mm may prove too difficult to work with. The 0.2mm is very fine, and while it will tolerate a reasonable amount of forceful handling, it can snap if treated roo roughly.

Hints on working with wire

- The size of each stitch or loop will be decided by the size of the hook or needle you use and some experimentation may be needed to determine which size suits which gauge wire. The type of project you are working on will also be a factor in your choice of hook or needle size.

- When casting on, use a loose slip knot and then slip this onto your hook or needle. Do not pull it tight as this will make it impossible to continue. For a knitting cast-on you may prefer to twist a loop onto your right-hand index finger and slide it onto the left-hand needle. Allow some slack in the wire as you do the cast-on row so that each stitch doesn't become too tight.

- Work loosely throughout the entire project! It's virtually impossible to get a needle or hook to slip through a tight loop.

- When crocheting, you are bound to occasionally lose sight of the loops of each stitch as you work each round or row unless you are prepared to work very slowly and very deliberately, forcing each stitch to sit 'just so' as it is worked. If you find that you are beginning to worry about your work looking less than perfect, remind yourself that you are working in a freeform manner and stop worrying about it.

- If you do prefer to work precisely, you will have to work slowly and, before commencing the next row, manipulate each loop of each stitch on the previous row so that it sits up and away from the 'fabric'. I have found with some wires that the loops tend to lean downwards, making both loops hard to see in the previous row.

- It is not necessary to pick up both loops from each previously crocheted stitch; just pick up a loop where you can and continue working. If you are working in a freeform manner it doesn't really matter.

- When making items with straight sides, such as the 'Crocheted Wire Amulet Bag', keep a check on how many stitches you have at the end of each row. If you find that you are one short or have one more than you should, just increase or decrease at the end of the row.

Working with wire has lots of potential. As with any new medium, practice is essential, but it's even more important that you experiment! This, above all else, whether you are using yarn or wire, is how you will gain not only confidence and proficiency but also make new discoveries.

Why not begin your exploration into working with wire by making the Crocheted Wire Amulet Bag, instructions for which are given below.

Fig. 90

You will need

Copper winding wire, size 0.2mm (available from motor rewinding shops)
or use 32 or 34 gauge (see 'Resources')

Crochet hook, 3mm (US 2)

Seed beads in main and contrast colours of your choice. **Note**: Any seed
beads can be used for this bag, but do make sure that you have enough
to finish it. I used roughly 650 beads for the main colour, about 200
beads in a contrast colour and 13 larger accent beads for the fringe.

Nymo beading thread (or other strong thread)

Beading needle, No. 10 (or a needle that will fit through your selected
beads)

ABBREVIATIONS

mc	main colour
cc	contrast colour
ch	chain
WS	wrong side
ss	slip stitch
dc(sc)	double crochet (single crochet)
htr(hdc)	half treble (half double crochet)
1 bdc(sc)	1 bead double crochet (single crochet)
3 bhtr(hdc)	3 bead half treble (half double crochet)
2 bch	2 bead chain

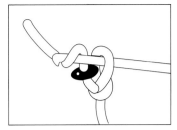

Fig. 91: bead chain

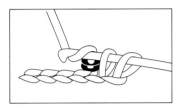

Fig. 92: bead double
crochet (single crochet)

Instructions

Before starting, thread 3 mc beads and 1 cc bead onto wire until you have approx. 120cm (47") of strung beads in a sequence of 3 and 1. Do not cut wire!

Note: Beads have a tendency to do their own thing, so always work your beaded rows from the wrong side so that they fall naturally to the right side.

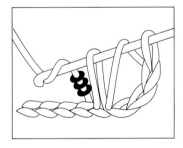

Fig. 93: bead half treble
(half double crochet)

FRONT

Chain 14.

1st Row: Starting from 2nd ch from hook, work one row dc (US sc). 2 ch, turn.

2nd Row: 1 htr (US hdc) in first ch, * 1 bhtr (US hdc) in next ch, 3 bhtr (US hdc) in next ch. Rep from * to last ch, work 1htr (US hdc) without bead. 1 ch, turn.

3rd Row: Work dc (US sc) to end.

4th Row: Work 1 htr (US hdc) in first ch, * 3 bhtr (US hdc) in next ch, 1 bhtr (US hdc) in next ch. Rep from * to last ch, work 1 htr (US hdc) without bead. 2ch, turn.

5th Row: Work dc (US sc) to end.

Rows 2 to 5 form pattern. Continue working these two rows until bag measures 6cm (2½").

6th & 7th Rows: Work dc (US sc) to end.

This finishes the front and folding rows of the bag.

Fig 94

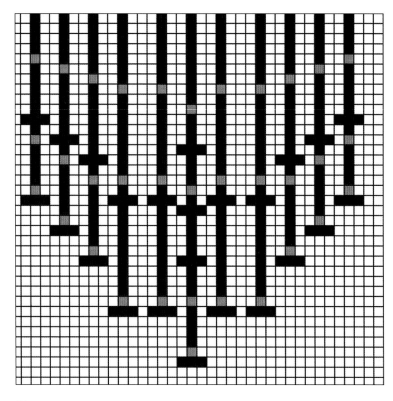

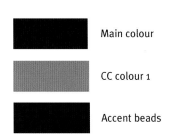

Main colour

CC colour 1

Accent beads

Fig. 95

BACK

Work in rows of htr (US hdc) (without beads) until back measures 6cm (2½"), making sure to finish on WS of work.

Fold bag in half at the two dc (US sc) rows previously worked.

With back of bag facing you, crochet the sides together as follows:

Work 1 ch, then, working through both thicknesses of the bag, work 4bdc (US sc) evenly along left side to bottom corner (10 sets of 4 bdc [US sc]). Work 2 dc (US sc) into the corner, continue along bottom edge of bag (8 sets), 2 dc (US sc) in next corner, and 10 sets of 4 bdc (US sc) along the other side of the bag.

Do not fasten off.

STRAP

With WS of bag facing you, work 1 dc (US sc) in corner of bag, then work * 2 ch, 2 bch *. Rep from * to * until strap is required length (approx. 66 cm [26"]), ending with 2 ch.

Secure to the other side of the bag with a slip stitch, taking care not to twist the strap.

Turn and work back along the strap as follows:

Work 2 bch at corner. * 2 ch, 2 bch in next ch loop *. Rep from * to * until the second side of the strap measures the same as the first, ending with 2 bch into the corner of the bag, next to the first strap.

Turn work so that WS is facing you, then along the top of the front of the bag only, work one row of 3 bdc (US sc) (11 sets). Fasten off.

To finish off any ends of wire, either cut them off flush with the bag, or turn them into an embellishment by twisting them firmly around a 3.5mm (US 4) knitting needle to make a tight coil. Remove needle and arrange into place.

FRINGING

Firstly, take a look at the lower edge of your bag and mentally work out how far apart each fringe row will need to be. You don't need to be exact — just make sure that you have enough spaces for all 9 rows of fringe.

Secure the beading thread to one corner of the bag by knotting it a few times around the wire.

String beads onto your thread, according to the graph in Fig. 94.

Run the thread back up *all but the three beads at the end of the row* — this creates a little loop and negates the need to tie off each fringe end.

Take your thread to the position of your next row and thread up the beads for this row.

Repeat for all fringe rows.

When the last row has been worked, take the thread as before up through all but the bottom three beads and secure it to the bottom of the bag. You may like to take the thread through several of the beads on the bottom row of the bag for extra security.

Knit Bead Amulet Bag

This simple little amulet bag is the perfect project for honing your bead knitting skills. Two stitches, garter and elongated, were used.

You will need

Small quantity of 4 ply (No. 8) cotton

Knitting needles, 3.25mm (US 3)

Crochet hook, 3.5mm (US 4)

Selection of size 11/0 seed beads (beads used must have holes big enough for the cotton to go through)

Accent beads for fringing

Nymo beading thread or other strong thread

Big eye needle or size 12 beading needle

ABBREVIATIONS

st(s)	stitch(es)
WS	wrong side
K1	knit one
yo	yarn over
3 bch	3 bead chain
2 bch	2 bead chain
1 bch	1 bead chain
ss	slip stitch

Instructions

See 'How to' chapter for instructions on how to knit and crochet with beads.

Fig. 96

FRONT

Cast on 12 sts.

1st Row: (WS facing) K1, * bring 1 bead up, K1, rep from * to last st, K1.

2nd Row: Knit.

3rd Row: As 1st.

4th Row: As 2nd.

5th Row: As 1st.

6th Row: K1, * yo, K1, rep from * to last st, K1.

7th Row: K1, * drop extra loop, bring 1 bead up, K1, rep from * to last st, K1.

Rep these 7 rows twice more.

22nd Row: Knit.

23rd Row: As 1st.

24th Row: Knit.

25th Row: As 1st.

Continue knitting for back of bag:

26th Row: Inc 1 stitch at each end of this row. **Note**: These extra two stitches balance the fabric to match the front which has been slightly reduced in size by the addition of the beads.

Continue in garter stitch until back measures the same as the front. Cast off.

Sew sides together using mattress stitch.

STRAP

With 3.5mm (US 4) hook, ch 1, *3 bch, ch 4, rep from * until strap measures length required.

Working back along the chain length just worked and with the WS facing, ch 3, 2 bch in the 2nd of 4th ch in previous row, * 4 ch, 1 bch in 2nd ch of 4 ch. Rep from * to end of strap. To finish this row, work 2 ch, then ss between the 1st 3 bead cluster to secure. Attach strap to bag, fasten off.

Note: If you prefer, you can knit the strap over 3 sts bringing up beads as required on each wrong side row.

FRINGING

You can follow the graph in Fig. 98 or design your own fringe! See the Crocheted Wire Amulet Bag instructions for how to attach fringing.

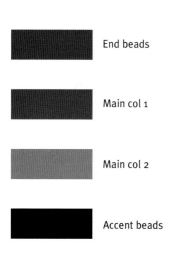

End beads

Main col 1

Main col 2

Accent beads

Fig. 97, Fig 98

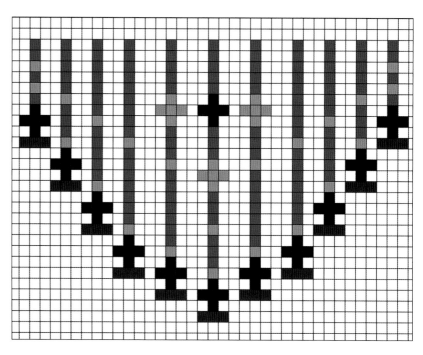

Ruana Collar

A 'Grow As You Go' Project

A 'grow as you go' project is one that evolves or 'grows' as you work. This eliminates the need for a tension gauge and allows you total design freedom – a perfect way to let your creative spirit soar! The collar in Fig. 100 is worked in the same technique as the 'Knitted Fragmented Strips Bag' but you could create any fabric you like from the ideas in this book since it is an easy project to experiment with.

To work the collar using the fragmented strips technique you will need to gather up at least 20 different yarns (more if you have them) in your chosen colour scheme.

Choose needles that suit the weight/thickness of your chosen yarns. If you want to use fine yarns in the mix, remember to double them to avoid 'edge creep', as discussed in the 'Knitted Fragmented Strips Bag' project.

The basic stitch used throughout is garter stitch, with loop stitch, wrap stitch, elongated stitch and eyelets from the 'FUNky FX' chapter. However, I mostly let the texture of the chosen yarns do the work and knitted most of the strips in plain garter stitch.

Before you start, you will need a template of the garment on which you will base your collar. I used a basic boat neck with square armholes (Fig. 99), which is possibly the easiest option since there is no armhole or neck curve to worry about, but you could use any of your favourite patterns as a guide.

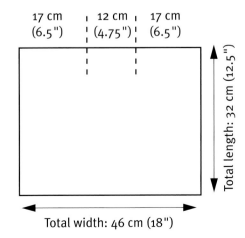

Fig. 99

Fig. 100

Constructing the collar

Decide how long you want your collar to be. Mine is 32cm (12½") and falls a little below the shoulder blades.

The width is determined by the width between your shoulder points. With a square armhole template, this is easy, as you just have to ignore the underarm extension and work with the width of the top section only, as is indicated by the red line in Fig. 101. The armhole depth can be used as a guide for the length of your collar but, if it isn't long enough, just add the extra length as required.

Since this is a 'grow as you go' project, you can now cast on some stitches for your first strip and commence knitting. You can choose to knit each of the strips in the correct length for the back of your collar or you can stop short of the total measurement and add more later on. It all

Fig. 101

depends on how you want to 'grow' your collar. Because you aren't working with a tension gauge it's almost inevitable that your strips won't match the template exactly.

The back of my collar was constructed as shown in Fig. 102. The arrows indicate which way the knitting lies in each segment and not necessarily the direction in which each was knitted.

Both fronts were single strips knitted vertically and measured 32cm (12½") long by 17cm (6¾") wide which, when stitched to the back, left a 12cm (4½") space for my neck. In other words, I didn't make the fronts exactly half the size of the back.

To finish off your collar, all you need to do is stitch the strips together, join the back to the fronts and add some fringing (see 'How to' chapter).

Fig. 102

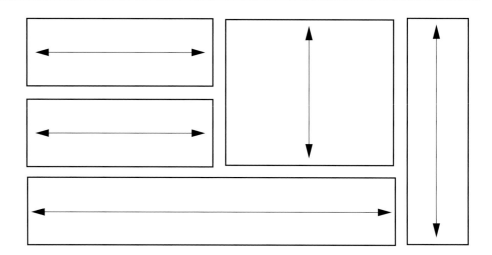

You have total freedom in the way you construct your collar and it's by no means necessary to follow my diagram, which is only one of many ways to do it. You may even choose to knit the entire back in one piece, pick up enough stitches at the shoulder edge for a front and continue knitting.

Fig. 103

The Scarf
That Grew

© Alison Vincent 2003

This garment is meant to be light and snuggly. It is also meant to be loose fitting and to drape over the shoulders, so there is no rigid structure, no shaping, no increasing and no decreasing.

You will need

There is no tension to work to on this garment so choose yarns that will give you a light, lace-like look.

The project illustrated here was made with 100g/200m (3½oz/220yds) of 12 ply (Heavy Worsted) mohair and 200 g/300 m (7oz/330yds) of a bouclé novelty yarn.

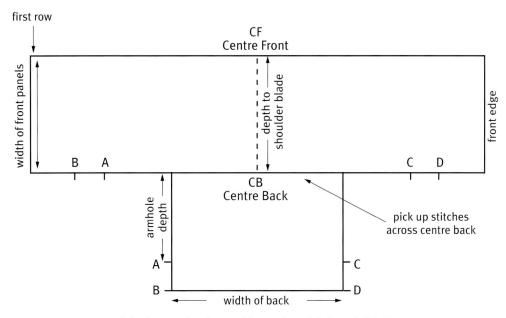

join front to back matching points A & B and C & D

Fig. 104: Schematic diagram showing how the scarf was constructed

Fig. 104a

Check the labels on the different yarns. If the manufacturers recommend using roughly the same size knitting needles, you can be reasonably certain that the yarns will work together.

To achieve a draped fabric, use a 6.5 mm (US 10½) crochet hook. If you are concerned about tension, work a small square, alternating the yarns you want to use and experimenting with the size of the hook — you may need to use a different sized hook with each yarn.

The idea is to use simple stitches and to let the texture of the yarn speak for itself. The only stitches used are dc (US sc) for the mohair strips and treble (US dc) for the novelty yarn.

Instructions — Part A

Before you begin, drape a tape measure around your neck and work out roughly how long you want the front edge to be. These instructions are worked on a length of 145cm (57") from the bottom of the left front to the bottom of the right front.

Use the bouclé yarn and work the required number of chains to give you approximately the length you desire. Remember that the length will vary once you work stitches into this chain so always chain more than you think you will need — any chain that you do not use can be carefully unpicked once the garment is finished.

In the example illustrated, I chained 117 stitches to achieve the length I wanted. If you make an odd number of stitches, it will make it easier when you get to part B.

1st Row: Starting with the third chain from the hook, work a row of tr (US dc).

2nd Row: Turn work, and with the same yarn work another row of tr (US dc).

Rows 3 & 4: Change to mohair and work two rows of dc (US sc).

I chose dc (US sc) for the mohair rows because that tended to make the colour more solid, but there is no reason why you shouldn't do all tr (US dc) rows with both yarns.

Part A forms the two front panels and the top half of the back. Work in the striped pattern, alternating two rows of dc (US sc) mohair with one row tr (US dc) bouclé until the strip is about 30–33cm (12–13") wide, finishing with a mohair row.

Now try it around your neck, draping it over your shoulders like a stole. Pull it up on the back of your neck so that the two front edges meet like a cardigan. Do you want to fold the edge over at the back of your neck to make a roll collar or just have it sit flat? At this stage, the back edge should hang to just below your shoulder blades. If you need to add more rows, just do one at a time and check the length as you go. When the strip is the right width, break yarn and fasten off.

To finish the back, you will need to pick up stitches along the bottom edge of this strip and work a straight panel in the striped pattern until the back is the length you want. Take time to think about this now. In my garment, the finished back is shorter than the front, finishing at waist length. Measure roughly how much longer you want the back to be.

The next question is how wide do you want the back to be? It should be just the width of your back; it does not need to wrap around.

From these measurements, I calculated that the back section, Part B, needed to be about 27cm (10½") wide and 23cm (9") long.

Instructions — Part B

1   Lay Part A flat, right side up, and find the middle of the last row. This is easy if you have an odd number of stitches. I had 115 stitches so the middle was the 58th stitch from the beginning.

2 Now you need to measure half the width of the back either side of the centre point — in my case approximately 13.5cm (5¼") either side of the 58th stitch — and mark with a pin.

3 Count up the number of stitches on each side, making sure that you have the same number of stitches either side of the centre. In the case of my scarf, 27cm (10½") approximated 23 stitches — the centre stitch plus 11 on either side.

4 Now join in yarn, keeping the sequence of strips, and crochet across these stitches. Continue in the striped pattern until the back is the length you want — try it on from time to time to check. Fasten off.

Finishing

So far you have a T-shape. To finish, you need to join the back to the front. More decisions! Try the garment on. If the back is shorter than the front, work out where you want the join to be. In my garment, the front is 1.5cm (½") longer than the back.

Work out, also, how long you want the join to be, as this will determine the depth of the armhole. Since I like to wear loose-fitting shirts, I wanted a deep armhole, and so I chose to make the side seam only 1.5cm (½").

Before you do anything else, think about how you want to join the back and the front. I crocheted the side seam and decided to put three small buttons on the front. You might want to use buttons at the side and a brooch or pin on the front, or you might want to make cords and tie the back and front together and do something similar on the front.

If you want to use buttons at the sides, determine whether you want the front to overlap the back or vice versa and where the buttonholes need to be. Similarly, if you want buttons on the front, determine where the buttonholes need to be.

With the right side of the T facing you, join the novelty yarn into the edge and dc (US sc) evenly around the whole garment, taking a little care with the edge down the sides of section B so that it doesn't become too wavy and uneven. Work the buttonholes where necessary and to the size required. You could choose to do this final edging in a contrasting yarn.

All that you need to do now is join the side seams and/or sew on the buttons.

If you want to finish with a corded edge or a picot edging, join the side seams first and then do the bottom and front edges and the armhole edges separately

Having made this pattern up pretty much as you have gone along, no doubt you have already thought about how you would do it differently next time.

This example was based on simple stitches and textured yarns. Why not use 'plain' yarn and textured stitches? You could alternate tr (US dc)

rows with shells, for example, or alternate tr (US dc) rows with rows of bobbles. I have used only two yarns, but if you have a good stash of bits and pieces, every row could be a different yarn or a different colour — or both.

Now that your garment is finished try turning it upside down. Put it on so that the side seams become the shoulder seams. One top becomes two — or just another idea for next time?

Note: This fun garment works equally well knitted (see Fig. 105). Use some fun yarns and large needles to achieve the draped effect!

Fig. 105

Zebra Bag

This bag is made using a technique that I think of as geometric scrumbling. The striped effect is achieved by using a variety of yarns, working in straight rows and changing yarn often.

Please read through the instructions before commencing this project to familiarise yourself with the technique.

You will need

Small bags, approx. 20cm x 15cm (8" x 6"), similar to those illustrated here require about 50 g (1¾ oz) of oddments of yarn. I like to make my bags with a plain back and use the same yarn for both the back and the edging. In this case you would need at least 25 g (approx. 1 oz) of the one type of yarn. As with all scrumbling, any type of yarn will do, provided that they are all roughly the same thickness. I prefer the majority of yarns to be roughly equivalent to 8 ply (DK), with some thicker and thinner yarns thrown in here and there. This weight of yarn made up with a 4.5mm (US 6) crochet hook produces a firm, dense fabric.

The 'zebra' look comes from contrasting two colours, but there is no restriction on the colour palette you can use to create an interesting effect.

You may need buttons to use as closures and material for lining (both are optional).

This bag is made in two pieces.

ABBREVIATIONS

ch	chain
dc(sc)	double crochet (single crochet)
dtr(tr)	double treble (treble)
htr(hdc)	half treble (half double crochet)
tr(dc)	treble (double crochet)

Instructions — Back

Fig. 106

Determine how big you want the finished bag to be. Start by chaining as many stitches as you need to match the width you require.

Tip: It is a good idea to make the chain slightly longer than you think you will need. Check the width again after you have completed the first row. Any chain you find you don't need can easily be unpicked.

Work the first row in dc (US sc) and then alternate rows of dc (US sc) and tr (US dc) until the piece is the desired length. Alternatively, you could work all dc (US sc) or all tr (US dc) — the choice is yours.

Instructions — Front

Using the back as a template, make a chain the required length to match the width of the back — the stripes will run horizontally.

Tip: Because working with different yarns and different stitches on the front tends to make the work spread, you may want to decrease the length of the rows on the front by two or three stitches. However, if the finished front is slightly wider than the back, this is not a problem!

The first row of the front is worked in dc (US sc) without changing yarn. For the second and all subsequent rows the rule is that there are no rules. Using the basic idea of crumpled stitch, i.e. alternating short and long stitches (see 'FUNky FX' chapter), work each row in any combination of stitches that comes into your head, with no more than any two adjacent stitches being the same. Add the odd bent bobble or popcorn stitch (see 'FUNky FX' chapter) here and there and change yarn frequently, say every 10 or 12 stitches, so that you get the striped effect and build up a wonderful dense texture at the same time.

1st Row: Worked in dc (US sc) without changing yarn.

2nd Row: 2 dc (US sc), 1 dtr (US tr), 1 dc (US sc), 1 dtr (US tr), 2 dc (US sc), 2 htr (US hdc), 1 dc (US sc), change yarn, 1 dc (US sc), 1 dtr (US tr), 1 dc (US sc), 5 tr (US dc), bobble, 1 dc (US sc), 1 tr (US dc), 2 dc (US sc), 1 dtr (US tr), 1 dc (US sc), 1 ch.

3rd Row: 2 dc (US sc), change yarn, 1 dtr (US tr), 2 dc (US sc), 1 tr (US dc), 1 dc (US sc), 1 htr (US hdc), 2 dc (US sc), 2 htr (US hdc), 1 dc (US sc), 1 dtr (US tr), 2 dc (US sc), change yarn, 1 tr (US dc), 1 dc (US sc), 1 dtr (US tr), 1 dc (US sc), 1 ch.

Make sure that you push all the lumps and bumps to the front of the work.

Note: It is important that you keep the same number of stitches throughout, so you do need to do a turning chain at the end of each row. Working with different yarns and different stitches it is easy to lose track of the number of stitches in each row. So that you don't get lost, it is a good idea every now and again to work a row in plain yarn so that you can easily count the stitches and adjust if necessary.

Tip: Work randomly, checking from time to time to make sure that the colour changes aren't starting to look too uniform.

Continue with the front until it is the same length as the back.

Finishing

1   Using a contrasting colour, pick up stitches and work at least one row of dc (US sc) evenly along the sides and bottom of the front, remembering to do three dc (US sc) at the corners so that the piece stays even and flat. If you want a wider border work more rows of dc (US sc) until you are happy with the result.

2   Now compare the back with the front. If the front is significantly wider than the back, don't panic. Work the same number of rows of dc (US sc) around the sides and bottom of the back, and then work extra rows of dc (US sc) down the sides until the two pieces are roughly the same width.

3   Next pick up stitches across the top of the back and work rows of dc (US sc) to make a border. If you are using buttons as a closure, the depth of this border will be determined by the size of your buttons. Otherwise, it can be any depth that balances with the border at the bottom and sides.

4   Work a border on the top of the front piece to correspond with the back, working in evenly spaced buttonholes if you want to use buttons as closures for the finished bag.

Fig. 107

Tip: If you want to line the bag, it is easier to measure the pieces now to get the dimensions for the lining. This will give you more accurate measurements.

5   Place the wrong sides of the front and back together. Joining in your yarn at the top right-hand corner, crochet the two pieces together with a row of dc (US sc).

6   Finally, make and attach a strap and the lining if required.

For the examples illustrated here (Fig. 107), I used upholstery fabric for the back of the bag. Cut a piece of fabric slightly smaller than the size you want the finished bag. Stabilise the edge of the fabric with a couple of rows of zigzag stitch. Then, using a large needle and the yarn you have used for the border, work an even row of either blanket stitch or running stitch, about 5mm (¼") in from the edge, around all four edges of the fabric. Using this row of stitching as your base 'chain', work rows of dc (US sc) around all sides of the back until it is the right size.

Variations

Variations

- For a fancier finish, why not add a picot edging to the finished bag?

- Joining the front and back together with a yarn that contrasts with the borders would add another original finishing touch.

- Think about which way you want the stripes to run — horizontally or vertically. To make the stripes run vertically, you need to work the front from side to side rather than from bottom to top.

- Think about how you might change the direction so that part of the front would have horizontal stripes and part would have vertical stripes.

- If you have lots of scraps of yarn, make both the back and the front striped — perhaps horizontal stripes on one side and vertical on the other.

Fold 'n Rolled Hat

These hats are fun to make and easy to wear. Basically, you knit a shaped rectangle, sew up a seam, fasten the top end, roll up the brim and it's ready to wear! You shape or curve the top or crown end by using short rows. The brim end also has some short row shaping to make it snug when rolled. Stranded garter stitch (instructions below and in 'FUNky FX' chapter) makes the fabric elastic and helps hold the shape well. The same set of instructions is used for the adult's and the child's version of this hat. In the child's version thinner yarns and finer needles are used.

Fig. 108

Fig 109

You will need

For the adult hats I used contrasting yarns and 5.5mm (US 9) knitting needles.

Yarn A for the brightly coloured hat (Fig. 108) is a multicoloured looped Burraweave mohair and Yarn B is a multicoloured Wendy Dennis 4 ply (Fingering) yarn — 75–100 g (2½–3½ oz) of each is plenty, with yarn to spare for trimming. Yarn A for the lighter coloured hat (Fig. 109) is a Collinette yarn, Tagliatelli, and Yarn B is a Cleckheaton 5 ply, Sportweight — 85–100 g (about 3 oz) of the Tagliatellli and 50 gm (1¾ oz) of the 5 ply (Sportweight) will give you yarn to spare for trimming. The weight of the Yarn Bs in both of these hats is equivalent to the weight of US sock yarn.

For each of the child versions (Figs. 110 and 111) I used two balls of the same yarn and 4mm (US 6) knitting needles. There is about 50 g (1¾ oz) of Fibreworks, 3ply (Fingering) yarn, in the brightly coloured hat and about the same weight of Littlewood Fleece, 4 ply (Fingering) yarn, in the paler hat. The weight of both of these yarns is equivalent to the weight of most sock yarns in the US.

Fig. 111

Fig. 110

Note: See 'Resources' for listings on where to obtain the yarns used in these projects.

ABBREVIATIONS

st(s)	stitch(es)
SG	stranded garter stitch
yfd	yarn forward (US wyif – with yarn in front)
YA	yarn A
YB	yarn B

Instructions — Stranded garter stitch

Note: It is advisable to work a sample in this technique before starting one of these hats (see below and/or in the 'FUNky FX' chapter). Bracketed sentence will need to change if we delete the technique instructions from the project

This technique involves knitting every row with two yarns alternately — we've called them Yarn A and Yarn B. These instructions will make a sample of the technique.

Cast on 20 sts loosely with Yarn A. Add in Yarn B.

1st Row: Knit YA, YB, YA, YB to the end of the row.

2nd Row: Same as Row 1. As you start each row, give both yarns a gentle tug to take up any slack involved in the turn.

Rows 3–20: Same as Row 1. Cast off.

In Row 2 and onwards you will notice that stitches that were knitted with Yarn A in the previous row will be knitted with Yarn B in the current row and vice versa. Those of you who have done Fair Isle or stranded knitting before will recognise what you are doing — except that there aren't any purl rows and the floats are short.

For those of you unfamiliar with Fair Isle, 'floats' are those bits of the yarn that sit on the purl side of the fabric between the stitches knitted with that particular yarn. Because this is garter stitch — every row is a plain knit row — there will be short floats on both sides and these can become a feature of the stitch, depending on the way the yarns are carried as you knit.

Lynne says:

I do stranded garter with one yarn above my right index finger and the other below. The one I carry above shows more prominently on the finished fabric. Sometimes I carry a textured yarn above and sometimes a smooth one — it depends on the effect I want. It's worth playing around using different yarns and combinations and seeing what effects you get and like.

Once you have your 20 stitch by 20 row sample you'll be able to estimate your overall gauge or tension.

INSTRUCTIONS — HAT

Cast on 80 sts loosely.

1st Row: Work SG (see below) to brim end.

2nd Row: SG to last 5 sts at crown end, turn (yfd), slip next st purl wise, yarns back, slip stitch back onto left-hand needle, turn. (This is called 'short row' or 'partial' knitting and is included in the 'How to' chapter.)

3rd Row: SG to brim end.

4th Row: SG to last 10 sts at crown end, work short row as in Row 2.

5th Row: SG to last 10 sts at brim end, turn.

6th Row: SG to crown end.

Rows 7–10: As rows 1–4.

Rows 11 & 12: SG to end.

Native Blossom Hat

© Lynne Johnson 2002

This is a loose-fitting hat to be worn over the ears, with the wider section of the band to the front, the side or the back, according to taste!

The band is made in stranded garter stitch (see 'FUNky FX' chapter) using two yarns, one smooth and one textured. The crown is made with short lengths of lots of different yarns, many of them highly textured, and the technique used is one I call 'shaggy reverse stocking stitch' (see 'FUNky FX' chapter). The colours and textures of the yarns, together with the shaggy reverse stocking stitch, produce a hat that reminds me of the blossoms of some of our gorgeous flowering native plants.

Fig. 112 (above)

Fig. 113 (left)

Band — You will need

50 g (1¾ oz) of a space-dyed 5 ply yarn (sock ply) for Yarn A

50 g (1¾ oz) of a multicoloured mohair, or mohair loop yarn, for Yarn B

Knitting needles, 3.75mm (US 5)

Gauge = 26 stitches to 10cm (4") both ways

ABBREVIATIONS

st(s)	stitch(es)
SG	stranded garter stitch
RSS	shaggy reverse stocking stitch
YA	yarn A
YB	yarn B
K2 tog	knit two together
dpns	double pointed needles

Instructions — Band

Note: It is advisable to work a sample in stranded garter stitch before starting this project (see the 'FUNky FX' chapter).

The band varies in width from 2–3cm (¾–1¼") on one side to about 13cm (5") on the other.

Cast on 10 sts (not too loose, not too tight) with Yarn A. Join in Yarn B.

1st Row: Knit YA, YB, to the end of the row.

2nd Row: Knit YA, YB to the last stitch. Increase in the last stitch by knitting into the front with YB and into the back of it with YA. (Increasing at the end of the row in stranded garter makes it easier to see how the next row starts.)

3rd Row: Knit YB, YA to the end of the row.

4th Row: Knit YA, YB to the last stitch. Increase in last stitch. Because the last stitch was a YB stitch, increase into the front of it with YA and into the back of it with YB.

5th Row: As Row 1.

6th Row: As Row 2.

7th Row: As Row 3.

8th Row: As Row 4 (14 sts).

Repeat Rows 1–4 until you have done 50 rows and have 35 stitches on your needle.

Rows 51–100: Do SG with no increases, alternating Yarns A and B as before.

101st Row: Knit YA, YB to the end of the row.

102nd Row: Knit YA, YB to the last two stitches. K2 tog with YA.

103rd Row: Knit YB, YA to the end of the row.

104th Row: Knit YA, YB to the last two stitches. K2 tog with YB.

Repeat Rows 101–104 until 10 sts remain. Cast off.

Sew the two narrow ends of the band together using a top stitch. This gives a nice flat seam.

Crown — You will need

Approx. 30 g (1 oz) of Yarn A or any other thinnish yarn for the base yarn

Approx. 40 g (1½ oz) of textured and novelty yarns (including Yarn B) for the shaggy effect

Set of double pointed needles, 5mm (US 8) or a circular needle, 5mm (US 8)

Instructions — Crown

The crown is knitted in the round. Knit up 120 stitches evenly around the increase/decrease edge of the band, with 40 stitches each on three of the dpns or all 120 on the circular needle. Place a marker after the last stitch if using a circular needle.

As mentioned above, I used shaggy reverse stocking stitch (RSS) (see 'FUNky FX' chapter) to get the plush effect for the crown. The RSS technique involves knitting with two yarns as though they were one — a thinnish yarn as the base and novelty and textured yarns providing the plush, or shaggy, effect. The novelty and textured yarns are cut into pieces roughly 15–20cm (6–8") long and are knitted one at a time with the base yarn.

About 4–6 stitches are knitted with the two yarns, leaving about 6–8cm (2½– 3¼") of them hanging each end of these stitches.

So that the hat would not be too heavy, I only added the yarn pieces every second row.

1st Row: Purl with the base yarn adding in pieces of yarn as you go depending on taste and interest.

2nd Row: Purl without adding extra yarn.

Rows 3 & 4, 5 & 6: Same as Rows 1 and 2. Place markers every 20 sts if using a circular needle.

Rows 7 & 8: As Rows 1 and 2 but decreasing 6 sts per row by knitting 2 sts together twice on each of the 3 dpns or once between each marker if using a circular needle. The decreasing can be done randomly or regularly.

As the number of stitches decrease those of you using circular needles may need to change to dpns.

Fig. 114

Continue decreasing at the same rate until 6 stitches remain.

Break off the base yarn and thread it through the remaining 6 stitches, pull it up and tie it off, trimming it to a length about the same as those of your shaggy pieces. It becomes part of the plush!

Enjoy your Blossom Hat!

Metallic Tunic with Floral Appliqué

Note: There is no tension gauge for this garment. Instead, you should use a template to check how many chains are required for the foundation row using the pattern instructions as a starting point.

You will need

150 g (5¼" oz) each of gold, silver, copper and black metallic or shiny yarn, 5 ply (US sport weight)

Crochet hook, 3.75mm (US 5 or F)

Beads of your choice for flower centres

ABBREVIATIONS

ch	chain
st(s)	stitch(es)
tr(dc)	treble (double crochet)
dc(sc)	double crochet (single crochet)
miss	skip
cont	continue

Instructions — Back and front

Foundation Row: Chain 124 (130, 136). Make 1 tr (US dc) in 5th chain from hook (counts as 1 tr (US dc), ch 2 throughout) * miss 2 ch, 1 tr (US dc) in next ch, repeat from * across row.

1st Row: Ch 5 to turn, * 1 tr (US dc) in next tr (US dc), ch 2, repeat from * ending 1 tr (US dc) in the 3rd ch of the turning ch 5.

Repeat Row 1, using several colours, changing colours every 4 or 5 rows. Change in different places on row, not necessarily at edges, to create the uneven striping effect. Work until 58.5cm (23"), 61cm (24"), 63.5cm (25") or desired length to shoulder. Fasten off.

Instructions — Sleeves

(Make 2). Chain 70 (76, 82). Work as for back until sleeve measures 25.5cm (10"), 28 cm(11"), 30.5cm (12") or desired length.

Finishing

Sew shoulder seams about 11.5cm (4½"), 12.5cm (5") or 14cm (5½") from outside edge.

Fold sleeves in half, set in place and sew in.

Sew underarm seams leaving a 10cm (4") opening at bottom edge for slit.

Embellishments

Make at least 50 flowers and leaves (more flowers than leaves), or as many as you wish, and stitch to top of mesh background (see Fig. 115).

Fig. 115

FLOWER

Chain 4, join with a slip stitch to form a ring, make 10 dc (US sc) in ring, join with a slip stitch.

Next round: * Chain 2, make 3 tr (US dc) in next st, ch 2, slip stitch in next st. Repeat from * 4 times more (5 petals). Fasten off.

LEAF

Chain 12, dc (US sc) in the back loop of each ch to last ch, 3 dc (US sc) in last ch. Now, working on other side of chain, dc (US sc) in next 8 dc (US sc), ch 1 and turn. Working in back loop, dc (US sc) in 8 dc (US sc), 3 dc (US sc) in next st, cont around other side, dc (US sc) in 8. End off. Add beads to flower centres.

Buttons and Closures

There have been many times when I have heard a knitter or a textile artist say that it's 'impossible' to find suitable buttons for their wearable art. We've probably all said that at some point in our creative life, and the simple solution is to make your own. This chapter will show you some of the ways you can use polymer clay to make stunning unique buttons and closures.

Before you start, please read the following basic polymer clay safety instructions:

Fig. 116

1. Always follow the manufacturer's temperature recommendation.

2. Always check your oven with an oven thermometer to ensure that the correct temperature is being used.

3. Never use a microwave oven.

4. Always clean your oven after each use.

5. Any porous kitchen items used in your clay work should not be used again for food preparation. All clay artists use items for their clay work only. If you should decide to work with clay on an everyday basis, it is also advisable to buy a small oven dedicated to polymer clay use. For occasional use, however, it is perfectly safe to use your home oven, but do give it a wipe out after each clay session.

Polymer clay fragment buttons

I love using polymer clay to simulate ancient artefacts. These 'fragment buttons' are super easy to make too. The tools required are minimal, and you can use your home oven to cure your pieces.

You will need

60 g package of white or beige polymer clay, or you can use dark clay and lighter coloured paints to create the 'aged' look if you prefer. Since buttons come under a reasonable amount of stress during their lifetime, I advise using a strong, flexible clay, such as Modelene, Premo or Fimo (see 'Resources')

Work surface: Ceramic or glass tile or small piece of laminated timber (a manila folder will work just as well if nothing else is available)

Textures: Your texture source could be anything you have around the house, such as old lace, jewellery, cutlery handles, print blocks, etc.

Small amount of cornstarch

Old baking tray, or ceramic tile lined with paper (baking paper or sheet of paper)

Wooden skewer or knitting needle for making buttonholes

Acrylic paints (Burnt Umber, Raw Umber, Raw Sienna, Cool Blue, Gold or Copper Metallic, or your favourite antiquing colours

Small amount of dirt (optional)

Tub of water

Small flat-ended paintbrush

Paper towel

Container of water for sanding

Wet and dry sandpaper in 400, 600 and 1000 grits

Buffing wheel or denim for polishing

Sealant: You can use any of the specialist polymer clay glazes or products available from the companies listed in 'Resources') or you can use Johnson's One Go, which is available from supermarkets, or Future Floor Polish if you are in the United States.

Instructions

Note: If you are new to polymer clay, it is *very important* that you check your oven with an oven thermometer to make sure that the temperature is correct before attempting to cure your items. Too low a temperature will result in under-cured clay and may cause your work to crack or break. Too high a temperature will result in fumes that are unpleasant to some people.

At the correct temperature, you will notice a slight smell. This is normal and, although perfectly safe, it is advisable during the curing process that you have good cross-ventilation.

Fig. 117

1   Condition your clay and roll into a roughly shaped ball. If you are new to polymer clay, 'conditioning' just means making it soft and malleable to use. This is done by breaking off small pieces from the block of clay and kneading it until it becomes soft. A good guide as to whether it has been sufficiently conditioned is to roll the clay into a fat snake and bend it in half. If it cracks, it needs more work.

2   Tear off a piece about the size of your thumbnail and flatten with your fingers until it is the size and thickness you want. I can't be specific because each fragment is different and they are not meant to match exactly. You will soon work out how much clay you need for each piece. Don't worry about fingerprints — these will be sanded off later.

3   To texture the fragments, lightly dust some cornstarch onto your textured source. If you are using lace or other fabric, brush the cornstarch onto the clay and then press the scrap of clay against the texture, flattening it to the desired shape and thickness and making sure that you don't use an area of texture that is fully representational of the image. That is, if you are using a spiral stamp, press the clay onto it a little off centre, or if it's a floral texture, as in lace, just pick up half the flower and a leaf or two.

4   Carefully remove the fragment from the textured source and place it on a baking tray or a ceramic tile that has been lined with paper. (I use baking paper, which is available from supermarkets). The temperature you will be curing at — 130°C (250°F) — is perfectly safe and the paper will not burn.

5   Before curing, however, you need to make the buttonholes. This is done by piercing the fragment with a knitting needle or wooden skewer. Pick the fragment up, push the needle or skewer through from one side and then from the other, being careful not to squash the textured surface too much. Fortunately, a little distortion to the shape won't really matter, since it will only add to the realism of the fragments. *Note*: A corn cob holder is worth getting if you can find one with points that are the same length, as they make perfectly spaced holes suitable for all but the smallest buttons.

6   Once you have made the buttonholes, cure according to the clay manufacturer's recommendation and allow to cool.

7   Once cool, you can scratch the surface of each piece with a needle tool to add to the antique look if you wish.

Instructions — Antiqueing your fragments

Now comes the fun and messy part:

1   Depending on the effect you want, choose the colour paint that best suits your purpose.

2   Wet your fingers and rub some dirt into the fragments, making sure that it gets down into the cracks and crevices.

3   Squeeze out some paint onto your work surface or a plastic lid, and with your paintbrush or fingers work it into the texture so that you get a good coverage.

4   Before the paint has time to dry, quickly wipe off the excess with some paper towel. If you were too heavy-handed with the paint, a quick wipe with *damp* paper towel will remove some of it. **Note**: Don't use running water because this will wash away too much of the paint. If you find that the paint didn't get right down into the depressions of the texture, use the paintbrush to get into those crevices.

5   Set aside to dry while you work on the other fragments.

Instructions – Sanding and polishing

1   When dry, sand gently with wet sandpaper, starting with 400, then the 600 and finally the 1000 grit. **Note**: You should *always* sand polymer clay using water to minimise dust particles. Sanding will remove some of the paint from the raised surface, so work gently if you don't want to remove a lot of the paint.

2   Sanding cured polymer clay results in a beautifully smooth, shiny surface and this can be accentuated by giving the surface a good polish. This can be done using a small jeweller's buffing wheel, which is the fastest and easiest way to do it. However, not everyone has one of these at his or her disposal. If you do use one of these wheels, you must wear safety goggles and a dust mask! A good alternative is to rub each piece vigorously on a piece of denim — it's easier if you are actually wearing a pair of jeans!

3   To protect your buttons you can now add a coat or two of sealant.

Moulded buttons

Here is another very easy technique for making buttons. Moulding buttons is also great fun. You can use old buttons or jewellery, shells, rubber stamps or any other small, interesting objects that you may find. It's better to choose objects without undercuts, as it's virtually impossible to remove them from a rigid clay mould.

Fig. 118

You will need

Scrap clay (only use your good, clean clay if you must)

Armor-All or cornflour

Small paintbrush

Baking paper

Rubber stamps, old buttons, charms, jewellery, etc.

Instructions

1 To make a mould, you will need to condition the scrap clay again until it's soft and pliable. Judging how much clay to use will take a little experimenting. You need to make sure that there is ample clay around the depression, at the same time not having too much excess around the outer edges. A thick original will need a fair depth of clay, say 2cm (¾"). Flatter objects don't need so much. Between 1.5cm (½") and 2cm (¾") seems to be the average thickness of most of my own moulds.

2 Brush a little Armor-All or dust some cornflour onto the original and press it into the prepared clay, making sure that you embed the entire piece into the clay. Gently work your thumbs over it to make sure that you reach all the recesses. Turn the piece over and press it down against your work surface (I always do this on some baking paper to

prevent sticking). This helps flatten out the surface of the mould, at the same time ensuring that the object is totally embedded. Now gently peel the clay away from the object. If it resists, gently lift one edge with your fingernail to aid release. If it won't release, it means that you didn't use enough release agent. If you aren't totally happy with the result, wipe away any excess release agent and try again.

3   Cure your mould at the recommended temperature, increasing the length of time by 15 minutes per 6mm (¼") if your mould is very thick. This will ensure that the mould is nice and strong. You probably won't need to cure for much longer than 45–60 minutes for thicker objects.

Now you have a negative of the original that you can keep forever. To make a positive you just need to repeat the above steps.

To antique or 'age' your moulded buttons, follow the steps in the polymer clay fragment button instructions.

Carved closures

Carving polymer clay is another of my favourite techniques. This involves transferring an image to clay and then carving and antiquing that image.

Fig. 119

You will need

Conditioned clay in the colour of your choice, rolled flat and cut to the
desired shape

Baking paper

Copyright-free image (see 'Resources')

Carving tool with a small 'v' shaped cutter (I use a Speedball, but any
carving tool will do)

Acrylic or oil paint

Small chisel-type paintbrush

Wet and dry sandpaper, 400, 600, 1000 and 1200 grits

Paper towel

Buffing wheel or piece of denim

Instructions — Transferring an image

In order to ensure perfect image transfers, the clay base has to be
perfectly flat and smooth. Dedicated clay artists use a pasta machine to
roll perfectly even sheets in a variety of thicknesses. If you want to
continue working with clay, I would recommend the purchase of one,
preferably Atlas brand. Imperia is quite good also, but doesn't have as
many settings as the Atlas. Look for them at kitchen supply shops or
stores such as K-Mart in Australia. However, if you don't want to go to
that expense, the easy alternative is to use two wooden skewers of
medium thickness and a smooth glass jar.

These are the steps for making carved closures:

1 Flatten the lump of clay as much as possible using your fingers.

2. Lay the clay onto a piece of baking paper between the two wooden
   skewers.

3 Roll the glass jar over the clay until it is the same height as the
   skewers.

4. Transfer your image to the piece of clay using one of the methods
   described below, or draw it directly onto cured clay with a soft pencil.
   Note: If your image includes writing or numbers you will first need
   to reverse the image using a computer paint program.

Method 1

Use a *toner*-based photocopy. Lay the image face down on raw clay and
burnish well, but gently, with the back of a spoon. Leave for 15–20
minutes. To check on transfer, gently lift one corner — if the image has
transferred, peel the paper off gently. The outline needs to be reasonably
clear to facilitate the carving process.

Method 2

Trace your image onto tracing paper with a soft lead pencil. Place traced image face down onto raw clay and burnish gently with your fingers. The image should transfer quickly using this method.

Instructions — Carving and painting

1   Cure the piece in the oven at 130°C (250°F) for 20 minutes. Let cool. You can begin carving as soon as the piece is cool enough to handle safely.

2   Don't carve too deeply into the image at your first attempt. You can always work over the whole image again if you want, but you cannot correct a deeply gouged area. Always carve away from your fingers as much as possible in order to avoid injury, slowly rotating the piece as you work. This rotational method works very well when carving circles. If you want deep, wide grooves you will need to use a larger 'u' shaped cutter. I only ever use the small 'v' cutter for this particular technique, but that is my personal preference. Some images, however, will have wider lines that will require a wider cutter.

3   Once you have carved the image, you can apply the paint, which will highlight the carved lines, following the same instructions as for the button fragments.

4   When you have applied enough paint, set the piece aside to dry.

5   When dry, you can sand the piece to remove excess paint from the surface, using wet and dry sandpaper. Start with the 400 grit, and then use the 600, 1000 and, finally, the 1200 grit. (See also instructions for the button fragments.)

Polymer clay is a very versatile medium for making buttons, jewellery and other items, and the techniques described here are just a few of the countless possibilities (see books in 'Bibliography' for further ideas).

FUNky FX

The special embellishments in this chapter will add a little touch of fun to your work!

They include a wide range of textural stitches and ideas for both knitting and crochet so that you will have lots of choice when creating your freeform fabrics. Some need to be worked over a complete row to achieve the full effect, while others can be worked on a section of a row or as the mood strikes.

Crochet FX

ABBREVIATIONS

Rd	round
ch	chain
st(s)	stitch(es)
tr	treble
dtr	double treble
ttr	triple treble
dc(sc)	double crochet (single crochet)
htr(hdc)	half treble (half double crochet)
tr(dc)	treble (double crochet)
dtr(tr)	double treble (treble)
tr tr(dtr)	triple treble (double treble)
ss	slip stitch
yoh	yarn over hook
WS	wrong side
RS	right side
beg	beginning
rep	repeat

dec	decrease
inc	increase

Applied decorative chain

Applied decorative chain (referred to as ADC in the instructions) is just a crocheted chain with textured elements added at any time as you work the chain stitches. It's a very easy way to create surface texture for your accessories or garments. Fig. 120 shows a hand-knitted garter stitch vest that has been embellished with applied decorative chain.

To work the chain, start with a number of chains. The number is entirely up to you since you may wish to begin your ADC with a textured element or a few centimetres (inches) of chain stitch. At any time, as you work the chain stitches, you can introduce one of the following textures.

CIRCULAR MOTIF

From the point in your chain that you want the motif to sit, work a further 4 ch sts. Slip stitch into 4th ch from hook to form a ring. Work 3 ch, then 13 treble (US dc) into ring (14 sts in all). Slip stitch into top

Fig. 120

of 3 ch to finish. This will create a flat motif. If you want one that is more cup shaped, only work 8 treble (US dc) into ring. Continue to work in ch st.

These are some variations:

- For smaller motifs work dc (US sc) or htr (US hdc) instead of trebles (US dc). For larger motifs work dtr (US tr).

- For an open work motif, start with 4 chains, instead of 3. Now work 1 tr (US dc), 1 ch into ring 8 times. Slip stitch to 3rd chain of beginning 4 ch to finish.

FLAPS

From the point in your chain that you want the flaps to sit, work 4 more chains. Into 2nd ch from hook work 1 dc (US sc), then work 1 dc (US sc) into next 4 sts. Work a few more ch sts then repeat. The number of flaps in any one section of the chain length is up to you. Continue with your chain length.

You can also use these variations:

- Work htr (US hdc) or even tr (US dc) to make wider flaps.

- Work 1dc, 1 htr (US hdc), 3 tr (US dc) to create shaped flaps. Experiment with this variation to create your own shapes.

BOBBLES

From the point in your chain that you want the bobbles to sit, work 4 more chains. In the 5th chain from the hook, work a bobble, as shown in the 'How to' chapter. As with the flaps, you can work a group of these together along the chain length or separate them with as many chain sts as you like.

IRREGULAR SHAPES

This is where you can let your imagination run wild. For a simple shape, from the point in your chain that you want the shape to sit, work 10 more chains. Working back along the 10 chains just worked, complete the following sequence of stitches.

Into 2nd ch from hook work 1 dc (US sc), 1 htr (US hdc) into each of next 2 sts, 1 tr (US dc) into each of next 3 sts, 1 dtr (US tr) into each of next 2 sts, 1 tr (US dc) into last st. Turn and work the same sequence of stitches back along the other side of the 10 chain section. Continue working your chain length to the position of your next decorative element.

To attach the ADC to your work stitch it down using a small running stitch.

The above ideas are just a few of many possibilities. Experiment!

Crocheted caterpillar braid

Make 2 ch.

1 dc (US sc) in 2nd ch from hook, turn.

* Insert hook in 2 side loops, yoh, draw through 2 loops, yoh, draw through remaining 2 loops, turn.

Rep from * for required length.

This cord can be used for bag straps — you need to use thick yarn and a size 5mm (US7) or 6mm (US9) hook for single straps, or 8 ply (US DK) yarn and a 4.5mm (US6) hook to make three single cords that can then be plaited together to make a more substantial strap.

As variations:

• Work 1 chain in between each turn and weave a contrasting yarn or ribbon through the resultant small holes.

• Work 2, 3 or even 5 chains between each turn for an interesting braid.

Fig. 121

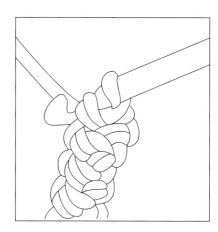

Fig. 122

Crochet I-Cord

Make 4 or 5 ch, ss into 1st ch to make a circle. Using dc (US sc) and with WS always facing, work round and round in a spiral formation for the length required.

I-Cords can be plaited together to make bag straps or used as surface decoration on a base fabric. Or thread thick cord through to make firm handles for bags.

Crochet flaps

Worked with the RS of the work facing, on a base row of dc (US sc), htr (US hdc) or tr (US dc).

Work to where you want your first flap to be.

1dc into st, ch 6, 1dc into 2nd ch from hook, 1 dc (US sc) in each of next 4 ch (flap made), * miss (skip) 1 st, 1dc (US sc) in next 2 sts, make flap as before, rep from * to end.

On the return row, work a stich of your choice into each dc (US sc) and one stitch into the space below each flap.

Fig. 123

Try these variations:

- For longer flaps make a longer chain row.
- Use htr (US hdc) or tr (US dc) instead of dc (US sc) for wider flaps.

Crochet triangles

Work some surface crochet using either of the methods described in the 'Crochet Stitch Collection' chapter to form a base for your triangle(s).

1st Row: At the position of your first triangle work 1 dc (US sc) into each of next 6 ch, turn.

2nd Row: Dec 1 st as follows (insert hook into next st, yoh and draw through yarn) twice, yoh and draw through all 3 loops on hook, 1 dc (US sc) in next 2 sts, dec 1 st, turn.

3rd Row: dc (US sc) in each st to end, turn.

4th Row: dec 1 st each end of row, turn.

5th Row: dc (US sc) in each st to end, turn.

6th Row: dec final 2 sts and fasten off.

Repeat as required.

Fig. 124

Triangles and flaps can be used at the lower edge of a jacket or vest to add interest to the hemline, or to add additional length. You will need to estimate the number of stitches there are available across the bottom edge of your garment and divide this by the number of triangles required. For instance, if you have 120 stitches and you want your triangles to be 10 stitches wide, you will work each one across 12 stitches. If you are one or two stitches under an even number, you can easily fudge the result by increasing in the first pick-up row of one or two of the triangles.

Cro-loops (also known as fur stitch)

Fig. 125

These can be worked over any number of stitches.

Use a ruler or cut a piece of strong cardboard to the size (width) required for the loops — 3–4cm (about 1½") is a good size, although you can use any width.

Base Row: Can be worked on any base row, such as dc (US sc), treble (US dc), etc.

Work as many base rows as required, turn.

Loop Row: Work 1 ch at beg of row. Place card against the back of the work with top edge just level with the last row worked (this will be the right side of your fabric). Starting with working yarn at the back of the card, bring it around and up between the fabric and the card. Insert hook into next stitch and, working to the *left* of the wrapped yarn, work a dc (US sc). Loop complete. **Note**: You may find it easier to hold the hook fabric and card in place with your right hand while wrapping the yarn around the card with your left hand, and then transfer the fabric and card to your left hand to work the dc (US sc) as usual.

Next Row: Work stitch of your choice along row.

These two rows form the pattern.

Work alternate rows of dc (US sc) or treble (US dc) between rows of loops to create a faux fur fabric, or if using as an accent only, work just one or two rows in any one area.

Elongated CroStitch

Fig. 126

This stitch can be worked on any base row. **Note**: The method is very similar to that of Cro-loops, but there are subtle differences, which help the fabric lie flat.

Work as many base rows as required, turn.

Work 1 ch at beg of row. Place card against the back of the work with top edge just level with the last row worked (the side with the card against it will be the right side of your fabric). Starting with working yarn at the back of the card, bring it around and up between the fabric and the card. Insert hook into next stitch and, working to the *left* of the wrapped yarn, work a slip stitch (ss) into the *front loop* only of this stitch. First loop is complete. Continue making loops to end of row. Fasten off.

Turn work so that RS is facing you. Make a slip knot on your crochet hook, insert hook into top of first loop and pull yarn through both loops on hook (ss made). Continue working an ss into each top of each loop to end of row.

Turn and work a row in the stitch of your choice into the *back loop* only of each ss in previous row.

Always work a loop row with the wrong side of the work facing you.

Here are some variations you may like to try:

- Cross each loop with its neighbour before working the ss for a slightly different effect.

- Use fancy yarn for the plain rows and plain yarn for the loop rows. You can of course use fancy yarn for the loops providing that the yarn isn't too heavily textured, as this may cause the loops to get lost.

Horizontal slit

Work until the position for the slit is reached. Work some chains (number required is dependent on the width of slit required), miss (US skip) the corresponding number of stitches and continue to the end of the row. On the next row work into the chain stitch loop previously worked and continue to the end of the row.

Fig. 127

Luxury fringing

This technique makes the most gorgeously extravagant fringing for the edges of garments or it can be used as a surface embellishment anywhere on a scrumbled fabric.

Fig. 128 shows strips of a patterned georgette type fabric that was torn into thin strips and then cut into 10cm (4") strips and connected to the base fabric with a dc (US sc) and a clever twist. The length of the strips is completely up to you, as is the width.

Fig. 129 shows the same fringing, only this time it was worked using a heavy chenille yarn.

Fig. 130 shows the use of 'silk curls'. Silk curls are also known as 'silk tops' and are available from shops that sell supplies for spinners (see 'Resources').

Fig. 128

Fig. 129

Fig. 130

Strips of fabric

Thick luxury yarn or silk curls cut into the required lengths

Note: If you are intending to work an entire yoke or panel in this technique, the yarn for the base fabric should be the same as for the rest of your garment, unless you do a separate swatch for a lighter or heavier yarn.

INSTRUCTIONS

This technique is always worked with the *wrong side* facing you.

Work a foundation chain of the length required for your project, or if you are working this fringing within the body of freeform fabric place it wherever you want the texture to be.

Work two rows of dc (US sc), turn.

1 ch (this ch does not count as first stitch), work 1dc in first dc (US sc) of previous row.

* Lay fabric length over work, from front to back, up close to the stitch just worked and *under* the working yarn.

Insert hook into next stitch, yoh and draw yarn through. Two loops on hook.

Take the end of the fabric strip that is sitting on the side of the work facing you (wrong side of work) and twist it up and around the hook so that it sits on top of the working yarn (both ends of the strip are now on the right side, i.e. the side facing *away* from you), yoh and draw through both loops on the hook, 1 dc (US sc) in next stitch.* Rep from * to *.

Work a row of dc (US sc) or htr (US hdc) between each row of fringing to bring you back to the wrong side.

How luxuriously thick your fringe is will depend on how many rows you want to work. I used four rows in the fabric strip sample, one row in the chenille sample and two rows in the silk curls sample.

Slip stitch cord

This is used as a surface embellishment.

Make a chain length to required measurement. Slip stitch into 2nd ch from hook, then into each chain to end. Fasten off.

The cord can now be stitched or couched to base fabric in a decorative manner.

Note: In all the following directions, any base row instructions at the beginning of a pattern refer to starting that pattern from scratch. In freeform work the base row can be anything at all, providing it gives you a suitable base to work from and unless otherwise stated.

Fig. 131

Vertical slits

Fig. 127 above shows both horizontal and vertical slits.

Work until the position for the slit is reached. Work several rows (number required is dependent on the length of slit required) on these stitche, ending at inner edge. Work in slip stitch down inner edge to bottom of slit, work across the remaining stitches for the same number of rows, and then continue across all stitches to complete.

Tip: You can have great fun with these slits or 'windows'. Try making a background fabric which, once stitched to the back of the overlay, will peep through the openings, or make little knots of fabric and stitch these to the inside top edge of the vertical slits so that they appear to be coming out through the fabric. Pick up some stitches across the top and bottom, or down each side of the slits, and knit a few rows of stocking stitch. The knitting will curl creating little rolls of fabric.

Woven crochet

For woven crochet you will need to create a base fabric or 'warp' of crochet mesh. For example, you could use a background worked in trebles (US dc), separated by 1 ch, or use dc (US sc) instead of trebles (US dc).

Strips of your chosen weaving fabric or yarn are then woven horizontally or vertically in a basic under and over configuration.

This is a technique with loads of potential. Experiment!

Fig. 132

Motifs

Although not strictly freeform, motifs can be very useful. They provide an easy way to cover gaps between your fragments after these have been stitched together; they are a means of disguising an area of your fabric that has perhaps too much of one colour or that may look a bit 'flat' and uninteresting; and they can be used very effectively as surface embellishment on plain crocheted or knitted backgrounds, as in Margaret Hubert's Metallic Tunic on page 116.

The simplest circular motif is a *treble circle* worked as follows:

Make a slip knot, then work 4 ch and join with slip stitch to form circle.

Work 3 ch, then 12 treble (US dc) into circle. Slip stitch into top of 3rd chain to close. Pull the slip knot slightly to close centre.

To attach circle to fabric, work a running stitch into the top chain of each treble (US dc) in the circle.

Fig. 132a

Combine the components in the following section to create unique and zany embellishments using some of your speciality yarns and threads. Be aware that the thicker the yarn used the larger the motifs will be. Add some beads for a little extra pizzazz!

FAN

Make 6 ch, join with ss to form circle, 1 ch.

1st Row: 6 dc (US sc) into circle, 3 ch, turn.

2nd Row: 1tr (US dc) into each of first 2 sts, 2 tr (US dc) into each of next 2 sts, 1 tr (US dc) into each of last 2sts, 1 ch, turn.

3rd Row: 1dc (US sc) into each of first 3 sts, 2 dc (US sc) into each of next 2 sts, 1dc (US sc) into each of last 3 sts, 3 ch, turn.

4th Row: (1 tr [US dc] into next st, 2 tr [US dc] into next st) 5 times, 1ch, turn.

5th Row: * (1 dc [US sc] into next st, 2 dc [US sc] into next st) twice, 1 dc (US sc) into next st, rep from * twice more, 3 ch, turn.

6th Row: * (1 tr [US dc] into each of next 2 sts, 2 tr [US dc] into next st) twice, 1 tr (US dc) into next st, rep from * twice more. Fasten off.

Fig. 133

SPIRAL SHELL

Make 29 ch.

1st Row: 2 dc (US sc) into 2nd ch from hook, 2 dc (US sc) into next ch, 2 htr (US hdc) into next ch, 2 tr (US dc) into each of next 22 ch, 2 htr (US hdc) into next ch, 2 dc (US sc) into each of next 2 ch. Fasten off.

Twist strip to form long thin spiral. You may need to coax the spiral into a shell shape.

Fig. 134   Fig. 135

Star flower 1

Make 5 ch, join with ss to form a circle.

1st Rd: 2 ch, 11 dc (US sc) into ring, ss in top of 2 ch.

2nd Rd: * 7 ch, 1 htr (US hdc) in 2nd ch from hook, 1 htr (US hdc) in each of next 4 ch, ss in bottom of ch, ss in back loop only of next 2 sts; rep from * 5 times.

3rd Rd: 1 dc (US sc) in each ch of petal, 1 dc (US sc) in each htr (US hdc) along other side of petal, ss in st between petals, ending with ss in st between last and first petal. Fasten off.

Fig. 136

Star flower 2

Make 4 ch and join with ss to form ring.

1st Rd: 3 ch (counts as first htr [US hdc]), 11 htr (US hdc) into ring, join with ss to top of 3 ch.

2nd Rd: * 6 ch, ss into 3rd ch from hook to form picot, 4 ch, ss into next htr (US hdc), repeat from * to end, working the last ss into the ss at the end of the first round. Fasten off.

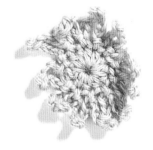

Flower

Make 5 ch, join with ss to form a circle.

1st Rd: 1 ch, 12 dc (US sc) into circle, ss to first ch.

2nd Rd: Working into *back* loop only of each dc (US sc), work 12 ch, ss into first dc (US sc), * ss into next dc (US sc), 12 ch, ss into same dc (US sc), rep from * to end.

3rd Rd: Work as for 2nd Round, but work into the *front* loop only of each dc (US sc) and work 8 ch instead of 12. Fasten off.

For variation, use a contrast yarn for the 3rd Round.

Fig. 137

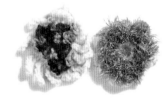

Fig. 138

Large leaf

Picot = make 3 ch, ss into first of these ch.

Make 15 ch and work as follows:

1 dc (US sc) into 2nd ch from hook.

Working 1 st into each ch, work 1 htr (US hdc), 3 tr, 4 dtr, 3 tr, 1 htr (US hdc), 1dc.

Make 3 ch, then working 1 st into each ch on the *other side of the starting chain* work 1 dc (US sc), 1 htr (US hdc), 3 tr (US dc), 4 dtr (US tr), 3 tr (US dc), 1 htr (US hdc), 1 dc (US sc), 3 ch, 1 dc (US sc) into 1st dc (US sc) at beg of round, 1 dc into next htr (US hdc), 1 picot (1 dc into each of next 2 sts, 1 picot) 6 times.

Fig. 139

Into 3 ch space at point of leaf work (1 dc, 4 ch, ss into 3rd ch from hook, 1 ch, 1 dc), (1 picot, 1 dc into each of next 2 sts) 7 times, ss into 3 ch space to finish. Fasten off.

You can omit the picot row if you prefer!

Small leaves can be constructed by starting with a shorter chain length and using fewer stitches for each side of the leaf.

For *large petals*, follow directions for the large leaf, omitting the picot row.

Small petals can be constructed in the same way as large petals by starting with a shorter chain length (say 10) and using fewer stitches for each side.

CURLY PETALS

Make 15 ch.

1st Row: Into 3rd ch from hook work 1 dc (US sc), 1 htr (US hdc) into next ch, 1 tr into each of next 9 ch, 1 htr (US hdc) into next ch, 1 dc into last ch. Fasten off.

Fig. 140

FLOWER CENTRE

Make 5 ch, join with ss to form circle.

1st Rd: 3 ch, work 12 tr (US dc) into circle. Join with ss into top of first 3 ch. Fasten off.

For a *smaller, more dome-like centre*, work only 8 tr (US dc) into circle. Turn dome upside down for a *cup-shaped centre*.

Fig. 141

FLOWER CUP

Make 4 ch, join with ss to form circle.

1st Rd: 1 ch, 7 dc into circle, join with ss into first ch.

2nd Rd: 1 ch, 1 dc into same st, * 2 dc into next dc, rep from * to end. Join with ss into first ch.

3rd Rd: 1ch, * 1 dc into next dc, rep from * to end. Join with ss into first ch.

4th Rd: As 3rd.

5th Rd: 3 ch, 1 tr into same st, * 2 tr into next dc, rep from * to end. Join with ss into 3rd of first 3 chs. Fasten off.

Fig. 142

For a *shallower cup*, stop at the 3rd round and then work the 5th round. Fasten off.

For a *deeper cup*, work two extra rounds as per the 3rd round *after* the 4th Round. Then work one round as per the 5th round to complete the cup.

LEAF BASE

Work 7 ch, join with ss to form circle.

1st Rd: 3 ch, work 13 tr (US dc) into circle, join with ss into top of first 3 ch.

2nd Rd: * 8 ch, 1 dc (US sc) into each of next 2 tr (US dc), rep from * 6 more times. Join with ss into first ch (7 loops).

3rd Rd: Work 15 dc (US sc) into each loop. Fasten off.

To make up your flowers layer the components, beginning with the leaf base, then the petals and finally the flower centre, stitching each layer as you go.

Fig. 143

There are many fun motif patterns available, so check out your stitch pattern dictionaries for more options.

Found objects

You can use any number of found objects to add that special touch to your work! Here are just a few suggestions: buttons; rubber O rings or lengths of plastic tubing that can be crocheted over and used as design elements in clothing, jewellery or wall hangings; fine copper or coloured wire; beads; raffia; strips of fabric; ribbons; feathers and felt.

Experiment!

Knitting FX

ABBREVIATIONS

Col	colour
dpns	double pointed needles
st(s)	stitch(es)
GS	garter stitch
st st	stocking stitch
rep	repeat
tog	together
RS	right side
WS	wrong side
YA	yarn A
YB	yarn B
yfwd/wyif	yarn forward/with yarn in front
yon	yarn over needle

Fig. 144

Elongated stitch

With Col A, cast on required number of stitches and knit 1 row. Counts as 1st Row.

2nd Row: K1, * yon twice, K1 * Rep from * to * until last stitch. K1.

3rd Row: Knit to end, dropping extra loops as you go.

Knit 3 rows with Col B.

The last 5 rows form the pattern. Rep as required.

The Scarf d'Opulence (Fig. 80) was made using this stitch.

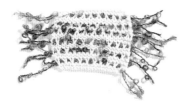

Fig. 145

Woven elongated stitch

Cast on an odd number of stitches and knit 4 rows in either garter stitch or stocking stitch.

2nd Row: K1, * yon once, K1.* Rep from * to * until last stitch, K1.

3rd Row: Knit to end, dropping extra loops as you go.

Knit 2 rows (the number of rows you knit depends on how close you want the woven strips to be).

The last 4 rows form the pattern. Rep as required.

The weaving yarn is woven in and out through the elongated stitches created in Row 2. Weaving yarn suggestions: wool tops (which can be lightly felted later if desired), ribbon, chunky yarn or several ends of an interesting yarn, heavy chenille, fabric strips, etc.

Fig. 146

Wrap stitch

This stitch is best worked on non-textured background fabric.

While it can be worked from either side of the fabric, work your first few stitches with the RS facing to get used to the process. Knit along the row to where you want the wrapped stitch to be. Thread a wool needle or bodkin with some contrasting yarn and insert it from the back of your work between the 3rd and 4th stitch on the left-hand needle, leaving a tail of approximately 8cm (3¼"). Wrap the contrast yarn firmly, but not too tightly, around these 3 stiches 3 or 4 times, depending on the thickness of the wrapping yarn, and then cut and tie off using a simple overhand knot at the back of the work. Continue knitting to the end of the row. Work a few more stitches and repeat. Or, if you are working over a small number of stitches, work one wrap only on each row, either randomly or evenly spaced, or staggered.

These are some variations:

- Wrap across more stitches to create a larger wrap.
- Tie ends off on RS of fabric, leaving a short tail to make a small tassel effect. You can also add beads to the tassel.

- Use ribbon, tie off on RS of fabric, and then tie into a tiny bow. You will need to leave longer tails for bows.

Vertical windows

Knit to where you want the window to be in the row, turn and knit a further 6 or 8 rows on this first group of stitches. Break yarn. Place these stitches onto a holder.

Join in yarn to the 2nd group of stitches, knit 4 rows and break off yarn.

Transfer held stitches back to working needle.

Join in yarn to beginning of row and knit across both groups of stitches, securing loose thread to the working yarn as you knit across the slit.

Fig. 147

For variation:

- Knit each side of the window in different yarns.
- Work windows at intervals across any number of stitches.
- Work the window fabric in a lightweight yarn and knit a backing of patterned or contrasting fabric to sit behind it.
- Use the 'window' concept to create purposely knit 'holes' in your fabric and decorate them with knots or flaps, as in the WhatKnot Vest, which is featured in the Gallery.

Horizontal windows

These are worked in the same way as you would make a horizontal buttonhole.

Knit to where you want your window to be. Cast off at least 6 stitches. Knit to the end of the row. Knit back to where you cast your stitches off, cast on 6 stitches and knit to end.

As a variation on both the vertical and the horizontal windows, you can pick up the edges of the windows and knit some stocking stitch rows that will form little rolls of fabric (see 'Stocking stitch rolls' below).

Fig. 148

WhatKnots

WhatKnots can be seen on the WhatKnot Vest in the 'Gallery'.

Choose a yarn that is not too thick unless you particularly want jumbo knots.

Cast on 4 sts and knit several rows on these 4 stitches until the strip measures at least 5cm (2")

Note: The number of rows is dependent on how heavy your yarn is. You must be able to tie the knot comfortably. Cast off (bind off) and tie the strip into a knot.

Try these variations:

- To make the knot appear to be coming out from behind a window, stitch one end of the knot tail to the inside top edge of the window.
- Make longer strips and tie two or more knots along their length.

Attached knotted strips

Attached knotted strips are easier to work on garter stitch or on the reverse side of stocking stitch.

They can be used as a randomly placed embellishment anywhere on the surface of your fabric. Pick up some stitches (how many depends on how large you want your knot to be, and is somewhat dependent on the thickness of your yarn) and knit a strip in either stocking stitch or garter stitch that measures approximately 5cm (2"). Cast off. Tie into a knot.

Fig. 149

Stocking stitch rolls

Stocking stitch rolls are easier to work on garter stitch or on the reverse side of stocking stitch (see also 'Horizontal windows' above). Use contrast yarn for maximum impact.

Pick up some stitches at the position chosen for the roll and knit several rows of stocking stitch. Cast off.

Note: If the first row *after* the pick-up row is a knit row, the roll will curl *up*. If you purl this first row, the roll will curl *down*. You may need to 'coax' the roll to help it curl.

Fig. 150

Garter stitch flaps

These flaps can be used to add length to a garment or as a decorative embellishment. Unlike stocking stitch, garter stitch flaps will not roll up. These are easier to work in garter stitch or the reverse side of stocking stitch.

At the position chosen for your flap, pick up as many stitches as required for the width of your flap and knit in garter stitch for length required. Cast off.

Fig. 151

Applied strips

These can be knitted in garter stitch or stocking stitch (see Fig. 152 and the WhatKnot Vest in the 'Gallery).

As your base fabric choose one of the following:

- contrasting garter stitch strips (the strips can be any width)
- garter stitch fabric in one colour
- purl side of stocking stitch strips
- stocking stitch fabric with a row of garter stitch at intervals of a predetermined depth, which will facilitate the even spacing of the strips

Fig. 152

- garter stitch fabric with a contrasting row at intervals of a predetermined depth

Applied strips look most effective when knitted in a contrast colour. They can be any width but look best when narrow, i.e. 5–10 stitches wide. You can work them evenly across the entire face of the fabric or randomly.

If you want symmetrically placed strips, divide your base fabric into sections that are determined by the desired width of your applied strips (for example, base fabric of 40 stitches = strips of either 5 or 8 stitches in width).

Instructions

Work the base fabric in your preferred method, making sure you finish with the right side facing. Leave the fabric on the needle or transfer the stitches to a stitch holder or safety pin.

With RS facing, join in the strip yarn to the right-hand bottom edge of the base fabric.

Pick up and knit 5 (or 10) sts from the cast-on row of the base fabric.

Continue knitting these stitches until the applied strip sits flat over the width of the first strip or pre-determined section without puckering or pulling.

Join top of applied strip to bottom of next strip as follows. Slip first st from left-hand needle onto right-hand needle, then pick up a loop from the base fabric where the strips meet, or from the contrast colour row, depending on which method you are using, and knit both stitch and loop together. Rep until all the applied strip stitches are joined to the base fabric (see WhatKnot Vest in 'Gallery').

Continue knitting and joining the strips until you reach the top of the base fabric. Place the strip stitches onto a stitch holder.

Continue knitting the remainder of the applied strips across and up the base fabric as required and, when completed, transfer all the strip stitches from the holder to a knitting needle, making sure that the right sides of both the base fabric and the strips are facing you.

With a 3rd needle (you may find it easier with a dpn), knit one stitch from the first strip with corresponding stitch from the base fabric across the row. Cast off.

If you want to place the strips in the middle of the fabric rather than starting at the lower edge and finishing at the top edge, join the strip in as already instructed but cast off at the same time as you attach the other end to the fabric as follows. Slip first stitch from left-hand needle onto right-hand needle, pick up a loop from the base fabric and knit stitch and loop together. Repeat with next stitch on left-hand needle, and then pass the 1st stitch over the 2nd as in normal casting off. Repeat until all stitches have been cast off. If you prefer, you can just cast off the applied strip stitches, leaving a long end, which you can stitch down later.

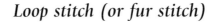

As a variation, knit a few extra rows in each applied strip, ending with an odd row (the needle holding the strip should be pointing to the left), and twist each strip once clockwise before joining to the next section of base fabric.

Experiment!

Loop stitch (or fur stitch)

Fig. 153

Cast on required number of stitches or use randomly in your work.

1st Row: K1, insert the needle into the next stitch as if you were going to knit it, keeping it on the right-hand needle and without slipping the stitch off the left-hand needle, pass the yarn to the front (as for purl stitch) and hold it under your left-hand thumb to form a loop, then back over your thumb and back between the needles. Knit into the same stitch and slip off. Pass the first stitch over the second to secure loop.

2nd Row: Knit.

Loops can be cut if you wish.

I-Cord

Fig. 154

1 Using dpns cast on 3–6 stitches and knit 1 row.

2 Without turning the work, push the stitches to the other end of the needle.

3 Knit, pulling the yarn tightly when working 1st stitch.

Rep steps 2 and 3 for length required. To finish, work a multiple decrease.

Maxi mesh

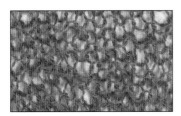

Fig. 155

Fig. 156

This can be achieved in a number of ways. One of my favourite ways to create this mesh is to knit Loopy Mohair or a similar yarn in garter stitch with size 20mm (US36) needles for a feather-light scarf or wrap.

A variation that would enable you to weave other yarns or ribbons through the mesh is creating a simple *eyelet mesh* as follows:

You need 12mm (US 15) knitting needles and the yarn should be a fine mohair or similar. This mesh can be worked over any number of stitches.

1st Row: K1, * yfwd, K2 tog, rep from * to end.

2nd Row: Purl.

Bows

Work to where you want your first bow to be. Turn work and * cast on 10 sts, then cast off 10 sts.* Repeat from * to *. Tie a knot to form the 'bow'.

These little bows can be worked randomly within your knitted or crochet fabric, or for a more uniform effect work them into your knitted fabric at regular intervals.

Fig. 157

Shaggy reverse stocking stitch

(© A LYNNE JOHNSON TECHNIQUE)

This stitch can be worked over any number of stitches, as in the Native Blossom Hat ('Projects'), or anywhere within your freeform fabric to add texture and interest.

Reverse stocking stitch — purl each row.

Cut the textured yarn into lengths roughly 15–20cm (6–8") long. These will be knitted one at a time with the base yarn.

Tip: Add the yarn lengths every second row to avoid making your hat too heavy.

Fig. 158

Knit 4–6 stitches with both yarns, leaving 6–8cm (2¼–3¼") of the textured yarn hanging at each end of these stitches, on the *right side of the fabric*. **Note**: It doesn't matter if these shaggy bits seem to be clumping together roughly in the same places — you will find that they tend to even out after a few rows.

1st Row: Purl with the base yarn, adding in pieces of yarn as you go depending on taste and interest.

2nd Row: Purl without adding extra yarn.

Stranded Garter Stitch

(© A LYNNE JOHNSON TECHNIQUE)

This technique involves knitting every row with two yarns alternately — let's call them Yarn A and Yarn B.

Cast on 20 sts loosely with Yarn A. Add in Yarn B.

1st Row: Knit YA, YB, YA, YB to the end of the row.

2nd Row: Same as Row 1. As you start each row give both yarns a gentle tug to take up any slack involved in the turn.

Rows 3–20: Same as Row 1. Cast off (bind off).

Fig. 159

In Row 2 and onwards you will notice that stitches that were knitted with Yarn A in the previous row will be knitted with Yarn B in the current row and vice versa. Those of you who have done Fair Isle or stranded knitting before will recognise what you are doing, except that there aren't any purl rows and the floats are short.

For those of you unfamiliar with Fair Isle, 'floats' are those bits of the yarn that sit on the purl side of the fabric between the stitches knitted with that particular yarn. Because this is garter stitch there will be short floats on both sides and these can become a feature of the stitch depending on the way the yarns are carried as you knit.

Lynne says:

I work stranded garter with one yarn above my right index finger and the other below. The one I carry above shows more prominently on the finished fabric. Sometimes I carry a textured yarn above and sometimes a smooth one — it depends on the effect I want. It's worth playing around using different yarns and combinations and seeing what effects you get and like.

Once you have your 20 stitch by 20 row sample you'll be able to estimate your overall gauge or tension.

Knit flower 1

Cast on 7 sts.

1st Row: Knit.

2nd Row: Purl.

3rd Row: K1, K2 tog, K1, K2 tog, K1.

4th Row: As 2nd.

5th Row: K2 tog, K1, K2 tog.

6th Row: As 2nd.

7th Row: K3 tog. Fasten off.

Make 4 more petals.

Sew 5 petals together at the centre (cast off edge, overlapping each one slightly).

With a contrasting colour, stitch a French knot into flower centre, or sew on a bead.

Fig. 160

Knit flower 2

Cast on 3 sts. Beginning with a knit row, cont in st st, inc 1 st at each end of the 1st and following alternate rows (7 sts).

Work 3 rows, ending with a purl row.

Next row: Slip 6 sts over 1st stitch on LH needle. Break yarn and pull through remaining stitch. Fasten off.

Make 2 more petals.

To finish: Sew 3 petals together in a circle, overlapping each one a little to form the flower. Stitch a French knot or sew a bead into the centre of the flower.

Fig. 161

Crochet Stitch Collection

ABBREVIATIONS

ch	chain
st(s)	stitch(es)
dc(sc)	double crochet (single crochet)
dtr(tr)	double treble (treble)
htr(hdc)	half treble (half double crochet)
tr(dc)	treble (double crochet)
tr tr(dtr)	triple treble (double treble)
yoh	yarn over hook
yrh	yarn round hook

Corded rib (or crab stitch)

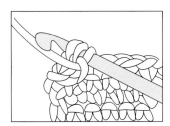

Fig. 162

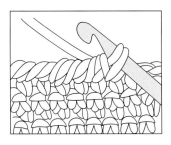

Fig. 163

This stitch is usually used as a decorative edging or textured stitch, but works wonderfully well as an isolated texture within your fragments. Stop at the end of a right side row. Do not turn, work one chain to give yourself working room, then insert hook into front loop of the 2nd stitch to the right, from front to back (see Fig. 162). With the hook pointing downwards, grasp the yarn and pull it through and under the working loop (not through the loop). There should be 2 loops on the hook. Yarn over and pull the yarn through the 2 loops on the hook. Repeat along row.

IMPORTANT: When working corded rib stitch in your freeform fragments, it is essential that you work into the *front loop only*, and not through both loops, as shown in Fig. 163 — you will need the back loop later to complete the effect.

Back raised ridge

This is worked around the stem of the stitches in the preceding row, but otherwise as normal.

Make a row of tr (US dc). Ch 2, turn. Mark as right side of work.

Row 2: * Yrh, from back of work, insert hook between 1st and 2nd sts of previous row and bring it out between 2nd and 3rd sts. Yrh and draw through a loop, yrh and draw through 2 loops, yrh and draw through last 2 loops. Rep from * along the row.

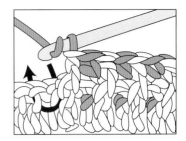

Fig. 164

Front raised ridge

Make a row of tr (US dc). Ch 3, turn. Mark as wrong side of work.

Row 2: * Yrh, from front of work, insert hook between 1st and 2nd sts of previous row and take it around the back and out between 2nd and 3rd sts. Yrh and draw through a loop, yrh and draw through 2 loops, yrh and draw through last 2 loops. Repeat from * along the row.

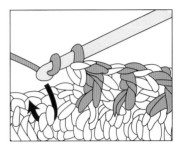

Fig. 165

Trailing stitch

Wrap yarn several times around hook, pick up a loop from the front of your fragment and pull yarn through this loop. * Yrh and pull through 2 sts, repeat from * until all loops have been worked off. Work a few stitches, then repeat. You can place these randomly or in 'V' shapes as illustrated. The more wraps you do, depending on how far down the fabric you go, the more 'wriggly' the stitch will be. You may find that your fabric will pucker if you go too deep with only 3 wraps, in which case you may prefer to undo this and add another wrap or two.

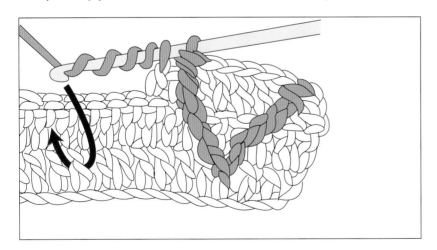

Fig. 166

Fig. 167

Fig. 168

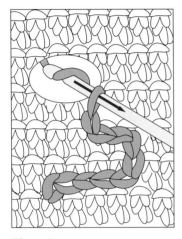

Fig. 169

Spiral

Work 24 ch, 3 tr (US dc) into 4th ch from hook * 4 tr (US dc) into next ch, rep from * to end of ch. Fasten off, leaving a long end for securing to project.

Surface crochet — Method 1

This is also known as **tambour crochet** because it mimics the process of tambour beading. This method was also used for the Meandering Shawl (Fig. 82).

Pull yarn through edge of fabric or tie yarn to edge of work if you prefer.

Hold working yarn behind fabric and insert hook from front to back through the first space between stitches. Pull yarn through fabric and the loop on hook.

Insert hook into background fabric again, pull yarn through fabric and then through the loop on the hook to complete another surface chain.

Repeat across fabric in any direction you wish to go.

Surface crochet — Method 2

Keep the hook and yarn on the right side of the background fabric.

* Insert hook and pick up a loop of fabric, yoh and make 1 dc (US sc). Rep from * for the required distance .

Tip: If you alternate the yarn from right to left for each stitch, you will prevent the row from slanting to the left or right.

You can now use this row of dc (US sc) as a base for adding triangles, flaps, ruffles etc. to your fabric.

Fig. 170

Fig. 171

Five treble bobble

Work to where you want the bobble to be.

Work 5 treble (US dc) into the same stitch, leaving the last loop of each treble (US dc) on the hook.

Yarn over and draw through all the loops on the hook. Work 1 ch to secure.

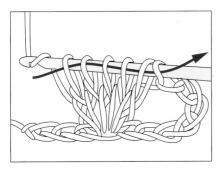

Fig. 172

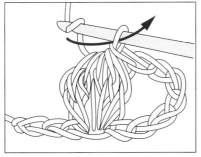

Fig. 173

Bent bobbles

Bent bobbles should be worked with wrong side of work facing you.

Work as for five treble bobbles (above). After working the 1 chain to secure, insert the hook back into the base of the bobble (the bobble is actually bending *away* from you) and draw the yarn through the loop on the hook (a slip stitch worked). Work a dc (US sc) in next stitch. In freeform crochet these bobbles are normally worked in groups of 3–5. If you work too many in any one row without spacing, you will find that the fabric gets wider and this may cause 'ruffling' in your fabric.

Fig. 174

Popcorn stitch

Proceed to where you want your popcorn to be. Work 5 complete trebles (US dc) into the same stitch. Remove hook from last working stitch. Insert hook through the top loop of the first treble (US dc) worked, then pick up the working stitch, yoh and pull yarn through.

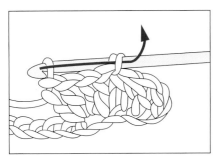

Fig. 175

Fig. 176

Fig. 177

Limpets

Limpets are normally found in Tunisian crochet but can be easily worked on a base row of any crochet stitch or knitted edge.

Proceed to where you want the limpet to be. Using the thumb cast-on method (see 'How to' chapter — the same procedure as shown is used whether you are using a hook or a needle), *loosely* cast on 8 stitches, yoh and pull through all loops on hook, 1 ch. Work 1 dc (US sc) in next stitch to anchor limpet to fabric and repeat for as many limpets as required.

Fig. 178

3D circles

These can be worked on a base row of dc (US sc), htr (US hdc) or treble (US dc), or introduced anywhere in your freeform work.

Proceed to where you want your first circle to be, then work 2 ch followed by 1 htr (US hdc) into the space between the next two stitches of the previous row.

Proceed as follows:

1   To work the first half of the circle, work 6 treble (US dc) around the stem of the next stitch on the previous row, inserting hook from front to back.

2   To work the second half of the circle, turn and work 6 treble (US dc) around the stem of *next* stitch on the previous row, inserting the hook from front to back as before.

3   Remove hook from working loop (taking care not to lose the loop), and insert it into the top of the first treble (US dc) worked in the first half of the circle, pick up the working loop and pull it through to join the circle. Then work 1 htr (US hdc) in space between next 2 stitches.

To do an entire row of 3D circles, you will need to space them by working several htr (US hdc) between each circle. To add to freeform work, position the circles as required.

Crumpled stitch

This is a super easy way of creating a bobble effect!

Work 1 dtr (US tr) in first stitch and 1 dc (US sc) in next stitch along the row. The shorter stitch makes the taller stitch 'crumple', forming a 'bobble'. You can work this stitch on either side of your work, but you may have to push it through to the right side of the fabric if it should want to fall the opposite way.

Experiment with different thicknesses of yarn.

Fig. 179

Chain loop pile stitch

This stitch begins the same way as the trailing stitch, but instead of working down into the surface of the fabric you work along the top of the previously worked row.

Wrap yarn 5–7 times around hook. Insert hook into next stitch on previous row, * yrh and draw through two loops. Rep from * until all loops are worked off.

Work a row of dc (US sc) between any two rows of chain loop pile stitch.

This stitch may also be worked as an isolated texture anywhere in your work.

Fig. 180

Ruffle

A ruffle can be worked on the surface of your fabric or along the edges. If you work it on an edge of a fragment, make sure that when you stitch the fragments together you stitch at the base of the ruffle so that it sits on top of the fabric.

At the edge: Needs a base row of either dc (US sc) or trebles (US dc). Work at least 6 tr (US dc) or htr (US hdc) into each base stitch.

On the surface: Work a row of ch st or dc (US sc) (see surface crochet above) on fabric surface. Then work at least 6 htr (US hdc) or tr (US dc) into each stitch.

Using a heavy yarn creates a deep ruffle. Unless that is what you want, it's better to use finer yarns or threads to achieve a more subtle effect.

Fig. 181

Roundells

These are worked on a base row of dc (US sc), htr (US hdc) or treble (US dc), etc.

Work to where you want the roundell to be. In next stitch work (1 tr [US dc] 1ch) 9 times. Remove hook from working loop, being careful not to lose the stitch, insert hook from back of work into top of first treble (US dc) worked, pick up working loop again, yrh and draw through both loops on hook. Work some treble (US dc) between each roundell to separate them.

These would look great as a trim around the edge of a sleeve!

Fig. 182

Flutterby wings (or lazy J stitch)

Make 10 ch.

1st Segment:

Miss ch nearest hook, over next 9 ch work:

* 1dc (US sc), 1 htr (US hdc), 1 tr (US dc), 2 tr (US dc), 1 tr (US dc), 2 dtr (US tr), 1 dtr (US tr), 2 tr tr (US dtr), 1 tr tr (US dtr) (you have increased 3 sts across row).

Fig. 183

Do not turn. Work corded rib back along row, inserting hook *under front loop only of each st.*

2nd Segment:

Work from * into 9 back loops behind the corded rib row just worked.

Note: If you make 10 segments, you will have created a wheel! Leave enough yarn to sew the 10th and the 1st segments together.

These are some variations:

- Vary the size of your segments by building a shorter or longer hill.

- Use a different colour for each segment.

- Work a full 10 segments and use for the crown of a hat!

Spikes

This stitch is good for disguising an area or adding a little more colour to a dull area. It can be worked from either the wrong side or the right side of your fabric in dc (US sc), htr (US hdc) or tr (US dc).

Proceed to where you want the spikes to be. Yrh and insert hook into fabric 1 row below, draw yarn through. Pull loops up and work treble (US dc) as usual.

For a graduated effect work each spike into the fabric at different depths. You can get an even gradation of spikes by working rows of dc (US sc) and working 1 row lower with each spike.

Fig. 184

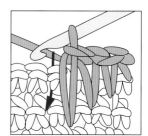

Fig. 185

How to

Thumb cast-on

Thumb cast-on works the same way with a knitting needle or a crochet hook.

Place a slip knot on hook or needle and wind yarn around thumb, as shown in Fig. 186.

Slide the hook or needle up along the thumb and under the loop, releasing the loop onto the hook or needle, as shown in Fig. 187.

Continue making loops on the right-hand hook or needle until the required number of stitches has been cast on (see Fig. 188).

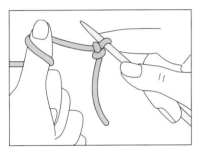

Fig. 186

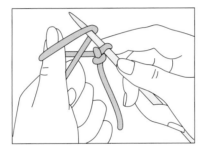

Fig. 187

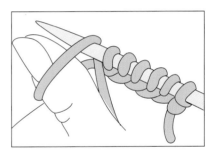

Fig. 188

Tassels

Tassels make great embellishments. Add them to the sides of bags, use as a feature on the back of a vest or jacket or as a design element anywhere on your fabric.

Fig. 189

Fig. 190

Fig. 191

1 Cut a rectangle of stiff cardboard approximately 10cm (4") long by 8cm (3¼") wide. Wrap the yarn around the cardboard lengthwise about 40 times (60 if you want a thicker tassel), as shown in Fig. 189.

   Tip: For longer tassels you can use a hard-cover book to wrap the yarn around.

2 Thread a length of yarn under and around the strands at one end of the card and tie off firmly. Leave the loose ends for attaching to your project. Cut the strands at the other end of the card (see Fig. 190).

3 Wrap a length of yarn several times around the tassel about 2cm (¾") from the top and fasten off, leaving long ends (see Fig. 191), which are then taken down under the wrapped section into the centre of the tassel. Trim tassel ends if necessary.

Right bias strips

Cast on 10 sts.

1st Row: K2 tog, knit to last st, increase.

2nd Row: Purl.

Rep these two rows for required length.

Left bias strips

Cast on 10 sts.

1st Row: Inc 1 st at beg of row, knit to last 2 sts, K2 tog.

2rd Row: Purl.

Rep these two rows for required length.

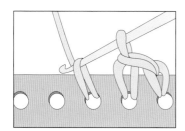

Fig. 192

As variations:

• Use garter stitch or moss stitch.

• While narrow strips of 10–12 stitches are great for covering unsightly edges, wider strips of 40 stitches or more make great scarves.

Leather and fabric inserts

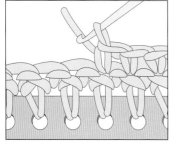

Fig. 193

These can be done in one of two ways, as below.

METHOD 1

1 Create holes in the leather or fabric pieces by means of an awl, large needle or leather punch. If you want an even row of holes, use a tracing wheel to mark the surface.

2 Insert a size 2.5mm (US 1) or 3.5mm (US 4) crochet hook into the first hole at the right-hand edge and draw through a loop. Work a dc (US sc) in the normal way.

Fig. 194

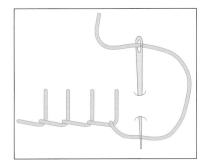

Fig. 195

METHOD 2

Make holes and stitch a row of blanket stitch around the insert and then crochet into the top loop of each stitch. This approach is easier to use when the insert material is stiff or inflexible.

Short row (or partial knitting)

This is great for creating new shapes within your freeform work. It works in either stocking stitch or garter stitch.

To practise this technique, cast on 30 sts and work 4 rows.

Knit until 5 sts remain on your left needle.* Slip the next st in a purlwise direction to your right needle. Take yarn to other side of work and slip the stitch back onto left needle. Turn work and continue knitting to end of row.*

Knit until 7 stitches remain on your left needle. Rep from * to *.

Knit until 9 stitches remain on your left needle. Rep from * to *.

To avoid the holes created by short row shaping, look at your sample with the right side facing and you will see a loop across the bottom of each of the stitches you previously slipped. To clean up the holes you need to knit that loop with its accompanying stitch as follows. (If you are knitting one row between each short row, as you work that one row stop before the stitch with the loop.)

Knit side facing: Pick up the loop and knit it with the stitch above it as shown in Fig. 196. Continue to the end of the row.

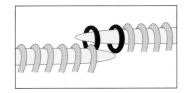

Fig. 196

Purl side facing: Pick up the loop and knit it with the stitch above it as shown in Fig. 197. Continue to the end of the row.

Note: If you are knitting several rows between each short row, pick up the loop from below the slipped stitch on the *first row* worked after the short row, and then knit the rest of your row sequence.

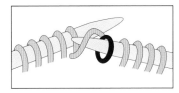

Fig. 197

Experiment with the way you work your short rows as you can achieve some fun results! Change the number of rows worked between each short row and play with the number of stitches worked before each short row turn.

Twisted fringe

Make any number of ch.

1st Row: 1 htr (US hdc) into 3rd ch from hook, 1 htr (US hdc) into each ch to end. Turn.

2nd Row (fringe row): 1 ch to count as 1st dc (US sc). Miss first st. *1 dc (US sc) into next st. Extend loop on hook for 10cm (4"). Hold stitch being worked with left hand and twist yarn on hook approx. 24 times in clockwise direction, fold twisted yarn in half, ss into top of stitch just worked. Rep from * to end, working last dc (US sc) into top of turning chain. Fasten off.

Tip: Hold twisted yarn at centre while working slip stitch for a better result.

Fig. 198

Fig. 199

Attaching a fringe

1 Cut multiple strands of yarn twice the length of the finished fringe. How many strands you use is dependent on how thick you want the fringe to be and on the thickness of the yarn you are using. Don't skimp on the amount used if you can help it as a skimpy fringe will do nothing for your finished item.

2 Divide the strands into groups of 4 or more and fold them in half.

3 Using a crochet hook and with the WS of the work facing, draw the folded loops through the edge of the fabric.

4 Place all the ends over the hook and draw them through the loops on the hook, and pull up tightly.

5 Repeat evenly along the edge of the fabric.

Mattress stitch

You work a mattress stitch seam with the right side of the work facing you. The technique works the same way whether it's knit or crochet fabric.

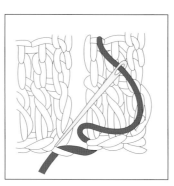

Fig. 200

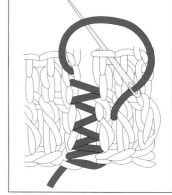

Fig. 201

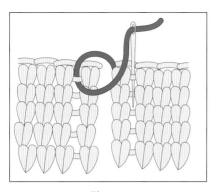

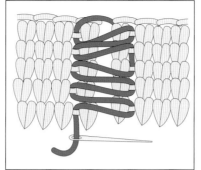

| Fig. 202 | Fig. 203 |

1 Place the two pieces of fabric together, right sides up.

2 Secure yarn to one side of the seam with two small stitches. Insert tapestry needle under the horizontal bar or loop between the two stitches.

3 Take yarn over to the other side and pick up a bar (knitting) or loop (crochet).

4 Every 5cm (2") or so pull yarn gently to close the seam. Continue alternating from one side to the other until seam is finished. Each time you close a section of the seam pull on both ends of the sewn fabric to help prevent puckering the fabric.

Beading

Before you start: If you are working from a pattern chart or in a certain design configuration, your beads must be pre-threaded in the correct order, remembering that the first bead threaded will be the final bead in the order.

TRANSFERRING BEADS TO WORKING THREAD WHERE BEAD HOLES ARE SMALL

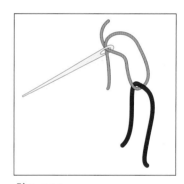

Fig. 204

1 Make a loop of thread through a fine beading needle so that both ends pass from either side through the eye. Loop the working yarn through the thread.

2 Slip the first bead over the needle, along the thread and onto double end of working yarn. Continue until all beads are threaded. Keep one bead over double end of working yarn at all times to help keep the yarn in place over the loop.

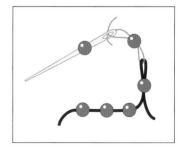

Fig. 205

TRANSFERRING PRE-STRUNG BEADS TO WORKING THREAD

1   Take care when removing strands of beads from the hank. *Do not undo the knot* or you will end up with beads everywhere!

2   Remove one strand only from the knot at the top of the hank.

3   Make a slip knot at one end of the strand, taking care not to drop beads from the open end of the strand. You may like to put a peg or other obstacle at the open end to prevent the beads slipping off as you do the transfer.

4   Thread the working *yarn* through the slip knot loop for about 12cm (4¾").

5   Tighten the slip knot until it is holding the working yarn firmly.

6   Push the beads onto the working yarn. Repeat with the remainder of the strands until enough beads have been transferred. It's always a good idea to transfer more than you think you may need for freeform work.

7   If you encounter a bead that has too small a hole for your working yarn, carefully 'break' the bead with long-nosed pliers. **Safety Tip**: Hold the bead strand under a towel before 'breaking' the offending bead to prevent injury!

Fig. 206

Tip: If you aren't working to a pattern and don't have pre-stranded beads, using a bead spinner makes threading the beads a breeze (see 'Resources').

KNITTING WITH BEADS

Garter stitch is the easiest stitch to use for bead knitting and is the method I've described here.

1st Row: With the *wrong side of your work facing you*, slide up a bead (or beads) after each stitch for a uniform row of beads, or randomly for a freeform effect.

2nd Row: Knit 1 row.

Rep these two rows as required.

Note: You can of course use beads with other knit stitches and you may like to explore this technique further. Montse Stanley's *Knitter's Handbook* is a good source of information (see 'Bibliography').

CROCHETING WITH BEADS

Note: In crochet, always work your bead rows from the wrong side so that they fall naturally to the right side.

BEADED CHAIN STITCH

Work a chain st, slide bead or beads down, yrh and pull yarn through. Continue to end.

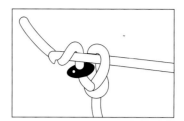

Fig. 207

BEADED DOUBLE CROCHET (US SC)

1st Row: Cast on required number of stitches. Turn.

2nd Row: 1 ch, insert hook in 2nd ch from hook and draw yarn through, slide down bead or beads, yrh and draw through both loops. Cont to end of row. Turn.

3rd Row: 1 ch, work dc (US sc) to end. Turn.

Repeat rows 2 and 3.

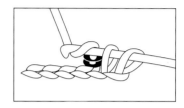

Fig. 208

BEADED TREBLES (US DC)

1st Row: Cast on required number of stitches. Turn.

2nd Row: 3 ch, yrh and draw loop up. Slide down bead or beads, (yrh and draw through two loops on hook), twice. Cont to end of row. Turn.

3rd Row: 3 ch, work tr (US dc) to end. Turn.

Repeat rows 2 and 3.

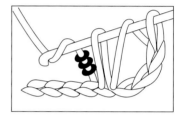

Fig. 209

Lining bags

Remember to pre-shrink any lining fabrics that may have a tendency to shrink when washed.

The general procedure for determining the size of the lining and inserting lining is as follows:

1   Measure the total length of the bag *less the length of flap if any*, and then add 4cm (1½") for hem.

2   Measure the width of the bag and add 4cm (1½") for seam allowance.

3   Fold lining in half and sew sides. Without turning inside out, insert the lining into the bag. Fold under the top 2cm (¾") of the lining and slip stitch to the top of the bag, just below the edge.

Note: I didn't line the flaps of my bags, but if you choose to do so, you will need to cut out a pattern to include this extra length and stitch the lining down accordingly.

Tip: For your fragment bags you can sew the fragments directly onto a suitable lining fabric.

Putting It All Together

Once you have created lots of fragments or completed some fragmented strips, you can start thinking about turning them into a unique piece of wearable art. If you haven't already made yourself a template, read through this section before proceeding.

Creating a garment template

To create a template, you can use an existing garment and draw around the shape directly onto your template fabric. **Note**: If you use paper first for the template, you will need to recut it using fabric, since a paper template won't hold up to the constant pinning and unpinning of your fragments or strips.

You can also use a favourite commercial paper pattern or a pattern-making software program such as Cochenille's Garment Designer, or one of the many others that are available (see 'Design' chapter).

For a beret, use a large dinner plate to draw the shape onto your fabric; for a bag, a simple square or rectangle of fabric is all you need. Experiment with different shapes!

GENERAL TEMPLATE TIPS

- You will need to check your template often if working in one piece (rather than with fragments) whether you are knitting in the 'Any Which Way' method or crocheting the fabric. It's very easy to get carried away when working this way, only to find that your vest or jacket front is too wide for the template.

- If you are working with fragmented strips and don't wish to bother with any neck shaping, just work straight strips that can then be turned back to form a 'lapel'.

- Use your overlocker to cut out the neck shaping and apply a bias strip (see 'How to' chapter) to hide the edge.

- For a simple top, a straight boat neckline is a good choice.

- For a jacket, a drop shoulder with straight sleeves is the easiest design to begin with.

Assembling crochet or knit fragments

Tip: If making a vest or a jacket, *always* work with both fronts at the same time to ensure a good balance of colour and texture.

When you have a reasonable number of fragments, you can start laying them randomly onto your template. I generally start somewhere in the middle and work outwards; however, there is no hard and fast rule about this, so do what feels right for you. If you aren't sure where to start, drop a handful of fragments onto the template and let them lie where they fall, adding and taking away from them until you begin to like the composition. If two fragments that perhaps contain exactly the same colour(s) in a similar quantity land together, you might want to move one. If two neighbouring fragments contain the same yarn, then one should probably be moved. It's all a matter of making sure that you have a balance of colour, texture/yarn and stitch structure throughout the entire garment.

Don't pin the fragments down yet as you will probably want to move them around a bit.

Tip: Sometimes a particular fragment will suggest a shape to you, such as the point of a vest front or the slope of a neckline. That's always a good place to start.

This stage of the process is a little like putting a jigsaw puzzle together, although the edges of the fragments won't 'fit' together in the same way as puzzle pieces do, and you may have to use a little ingenuity to get some of them to behave.

I'll give you tips later in this chapter on how to solve some of the problems you may encounter.

Keep moving the fragments around on the template until you are completely happy with the way they are looking. Once they are positioned to your satisfaction, pin them down.

Fig. 210

WHAT ABOUT ALL THE EMPTY SPACE?

How many 'fragments' you started with will determine how much space there is around the edges of your work. If you made a lot of fragments before putting them onto the template, chances are that you won't have much filling in to do at all, except around the very edges. In fact it's possible that you may find you have too many fragments, or that some are too big to be useful, especially as you get near the edges. Don't worry — they can be used in another project, such as a hat or a bag.

Here are some useful tips:

- For any larger gaps you have at the edge, you can create more fragments to fit the spaces. A good tip is to lay a sheet of paper in the gap area, and draw around the 'empty' area. You can then use this as a little template.

- For smaller gaps at the edges, it's easier to fill them in after you have stitched all the main fragments together. This can be done in a variety of ways, the easiest being to work some dc (US sc), htr (US hdc) or treble (US dc) into the area. Small, straight gaps are easy in that a row of suitable stitches of an appropriate height will do the job.

- Curved or 'V' shaped spaces will require a variation in the height of the stitches used. To fill a 'V' shaped gap, start at the very bottom of the 'V' with a dc (US sc) and then work a slip stitch into the side of the 'V'. Turn and work 2 dc (US sc) (or however many it requires) back along the row and work a slip stitch into the other side of the 'V'. Turn and work some treble (US dc) across the row, once again slip stitching into the other side of the 'V'. Continue working this way until the gap is filled. If you find you've worked too many stitches and have 'ruffled' the fabric, it's not always necessary to undo it — just fold or pleat the fabric until it sits flat and stitch it down.

- To fill a curved gap, start at one side of the gap and work a row of stitches, beginning with the shortest stitch, i.e. a dc (US sc), gradually increasing the height until you reach the centre of the curve, and then reversing the sequence to finish filling the space.

- It would be very unusual if you were able to avoid at least one small gap somewhere in the middle of your work because the fragments you make aren't constructed to fit together perfectly. Some solutions are:

  Work some stitches as described for the outer edges.

  Work bridges of chain stitch across the gap.

  Make a little treble (US dc) circle and stitch that over the gap.

  Knit or crochet a separate triangle and stitch that down to cover the gap.

IF IT DOESN'T FEEL QUITE RIGHT ...

The process of assembling your fragments onto your template will become easier with experience. If, when you've finished, it doesn't feel quite right, try the following tips:

- Leave the project for a few hours, or even a day or two, and come back to it with fresh eyes.

- If possible, leave it where you can see it each day, as it's quite usual for an obvious solution to come to you when you least expect it.

- Prop it up somewhere so that you can stand well back from it, and even turn it upside down to get a different perspective.

STITCHING THE FRAGMENTS TOGETHER

Once you are perfectly happy with how everything looks, you can begin stitching the fragments together. Note that during the 'stitching together process', the fragments will bunch up a little. The reason for this is that the act of stitching them together causes them to take up less space on the template. You will find that you will need to undo the pins from time to time to accommodate this.

This 'bunching up' will also cause the empty spaces around the edges to become larger. This is easily fixed by making some smaller fragments. As mentioned previously, using a tiny paper template as a guide makes this easier, or you can pick up the garment piece, still pinned to the template, and work some rows of suitable stitches directly onto it.

Tip: If at any time you find two fragments are crowding each other, overlapping one with the other, or holding the sides together and crocheting them together, will force them to share the same space. Conversely, if two fragments don't quite fit together, you can either fill in the gap with some dc (US sc) or make a treble (US dc) circle to sew over it.

If a fragment is too big for the space, you can do one of the following:

- Overlap one edge onto or under an adjoining fragment and stitch down with a back stitch, slip stitch or embroidery chain stitch.

- Hold the edges of the 'too large' fragment and its adjoining fragment with wrong sides together and crochet them together. The resultant ridge will become 'just another texture'.

TIPS FOR SEWING THE FRAGMENTS TOGETHER

- Leave the fragments pinned to the template for as long as you can as this will make the process easier.

- Choose a reasonably strong, and preferably plain yarn from the selection used in your project for your stitching thread — one that blends in reasonably well with the other yarns used is the best choice.

- With the right side of the work facing, stitch the fragments together with an evenly spaced overhand stitch.

If at any time you find two fragments are crowding each other, you can force them to share the same space by using either of the following two methods:

- Overlap one with the other, then stitch through them using a backstitch, running stitch or crochet chain.

or

- Hold the wrong sides of the two fragments together and crochet through them — the resultant ridge will become just another texture.

- Conversely, if two fragments don't quite fit together, you can either fill in the gap with some dc (US sc) or make a treble (US dc) circle to sew over it.

- If you have worked bobbles on the edge of a fragment, hold them out of the way and stitch into the 'backs' of the bobbles. This ensures that they will sit on top of the fabric and will not disappear into it.

- If you have worked a ruffle on the edge of a fragment, catch a loop from below the ruffle so that it sits on top of the fabric.

UH, OH ... HOW DID THAT HAPPEN?

Sometimes, no matter how careful you might be during the construction process, you might find an area that you are not happy with once it's all stitched together. It might be that a colour is screaming at you — How did *that* get in there? Or perhaps there is a large, flat area that sticks out like a sore thumb, or one area of a colour is just too big.

Fortunately, all these are very easy to fix! Here are just a few ideas:

- Choose an appropriate yarn (in colour and texture) and work some surface crochet over the offending area.

- Make a treble (US dc) circle and attach it to the problem area.

- Weave some contrasting yarn through the area.

- Pick up some stitches from the surface of the area and knit some little flaps or triangles in a contrast colour.

Experiment! Ask yourself 'what if?' — there are many ways to disguise a problem area!

Tip: If you introduce something new, whether it is colour or texture, you may like to add one or two of the same design elements to other areas to maintain a sense of overall unity and balance.

Sewing freeform garments together

To join the side seams of a scrumbled garment, use mattress stitch, as explained in the 'How to' chapter. This makes an invisible seam on the right side of your work and a ridge on the wrong side. Don't discount the possibility of using this ridge as a design element!

Using a template for fragmented strips fabric

The Ruana Collar in the 'Projects' chapter is an example of this technique.

Once you have several strips finished, use your template as a guide to see how things are looking. Lay them onto the template, moving them around until you are happy with the arrangement. Now comes the fun part! It's highly likely that you won't actually fluke it and end up with 10 strips that fit your template width exactly. You may end up with a gap of just, say, 2cm (¾"), and finding a creative solution to the problem will be your challenge. For such a small gap, edging each piece with a row of dc (US sc) in a contrasting yarn will do the job.

Here are some other suggestions as well:

- For a bigger gap, you could 'join' the strips using a crocheted mesh stitch.

- You could knit or crochet a narrow braid with which to join the strips.

- If you want to add a feature that really stands out, make fewer strips than you need, and then add strips constructed using a totally different technique or a different fabric, such as leather or a woven fabric of a suitable weight.

- If the sides of the strips are 'bumpy' because you have used a thicker yarn in places, don't worry about trying to hide this; instead, use it to your advantage by turning it into another textured design element. When you stitch the strips together, fold the wider bumpy section to the front, and stitch behind it, so that the bump sits in front of the seam. You can eliminate this 'bumpy edge' problem somewhat by using finer yarns.

- Add short rows of dc (US sc) to even out the sides of the strips.

- For strips that are too short, you can add a yoke, again using a totally different technique or fabric to that used for the strips.

- If you don't want to use a yoke, add triangles or long strips of knitted/crocheted fabric to the hemline to add length.

There are many different ideas you can use to finish off your fragmented strips projects, some of which you will find in the 'FUNky FX' chapter.

Using your template as a permanent lining

Lining freeform garments doesn't seem to be necessary and it is not something that I ever do, with the exception of bags. It appears that the various directions the fabric takes after the fragments have been assembled has a stabilising effect on the final garment. This, for me, is another huge plus for this wonderful freeform technique!

If you do want to line your work, the usual way is to cut and sew the lining from a special lining fabric. Another simpler approach is to do what Margaret Hubert from the US sometimes does, and that is to stitch your fragments directly onto a suitable fabric. In her Freeform video (see introduction to 'Projects'), Margaret uses a shop bought fleecy top, cuts it up the middle to turn it into a jacket and stitches her fragments straight onto it. She then covers the two front edges with a binding. Perhaps in our Australian climate using this would not be quite so practical, but the idea is a great one for those who do like to line their garments. Margaret also uses this lining technique for her freeform bags.

The 'Grow As You Go' technique for garments

AIM

To create a stunning piece of wearable art while avoiding a tension gauge at all costs and to complete it within a three-week time frame.

PROCESS

1   Begin with just a vague idea in your head of what your finished garment might be. A scrumbled jacket? A vest? You have plenty of vests — a coat perhaps? You decide to be semi-adventurous and go for the jacket.

2   Choose your colour scheme and start scrumbling some fragments.

3   Start to panic because the event to which you want to wear your garment is only two weeks away. No way will you be able to scrumble an entire jacket in this time unless you don't eat, sleep or shower!

4   Change to the easier vest option. Time remains a problem!

5   Think 'Why did I choose these bright colours?' and 'Where did those last three days go?'

6   Event is now just 10 days away and you only have enough fragments for one vest front! And why did you choose these colours?

7   Panic!

8   Decide that there is no way you could possibly wear an entire vest in these bright colours.

Fig 211

9 Refer to Plan B if you have one. If not, it's time you did.

10 There are enough fragments to make a yoke, which you know you can get away with wearing, even in these bright colours, so proceed to assemble said yoke. The vest once again reverts to a jacket since there is now time to knit or crochet the body and sleeves in black. This will help 'tone' down the brightness.

11 Pat yourself on the back. Problem solved.

12 Refer to template and make enough chains for length of jacket body. Treble (US dc) sideways until back and two fronts are finished. Just six days to go!

Fig 212

13 Attach body to yoke. Try on.

14 Panic! It's too short!

15 Think! Light bulb goes on! Employ the 'Grow As You Go' technique.

16 Time is running out so utilise a fast technique. Obviously it has to be garter stitch using largish needles — one slightly bigger than the other. Pick up stitches across back section and knit furiously. Try on. It's now long enough. Repeat for fronts.

17 With still five days to go, there is enough time to crochet the sleeves using a template as a shaping guide. Mission accomplished and there are still three and a half days to go.

18 Try on. Hmmm ... bright yoke ... dull body. AND the sleeves are a tad short.

19 Don't panic yet. Think hard instead. Knit some garter stitch rows to 'grow' the sleeves while thinking about what will match the body, making it look as though the add-on borders were always meant to be. Light bulb goes on once again as eyes light on some recently purchased sari silk yarn in stash. The colours match the yoke!

20 Weave sari silk through every 4th row of trebles in body sections. No time to weave in all the ends so just let them hang loose. Looks great!

21 Try on again. At least it fits now, although those garter stitch borders on the sleeves look too ... well ... black.

22 Make coffee and eat cake while you ponder. Weaving won't work again ... too much of the vertical. Light bulb explodes!

23 Couch sari silk in between garter stitch rows on sleeve borders. Repeat on jacket borders. No time to weave in the ends so leave them to hang. Perfect!

24 Sew on some buttons, try on and admire!

Despite the above story being a humorous description of how this jacket was made, creating garments using this method does require a little ingenuity and a lot of 'free' thinking. But it's great fun and the results can be very rewarding.

It's Time to
Spread Your Wings

I n the preceding chapters you learned a lot of new and fun techniques that I hope have inspired you to be more adventurous in your work, to take some chances, to think outside the square, to take what you've learned and create a style that is uniquely you!

In the 'Fragments' chapter, I emphasised that those patterns were to be seen only as a means to an end, and not as the only way to create scrumbled or freeform fabric.

Now that you have a grasp of the scrumbling concept perhaps you would like the challenge of working in larger pieces, rather than with fragments, or of creating fabric using just one favourite textured stitch together with the basic stitches (see 'Tracks' in the 'Gallery'). The fabric in this shawl is made up of trebles (US dc), half trebles (US hdc), and just one textured stitch, the corded rib stitch. Or perhaps you would like to try the 'Grow As You Go' method. You are what makes your art unique, so whichever way your creative endeavours may lead you always remember the following:

If you hear a different drummer dreamer, take a chance.

The road you choose to travel means the difference in the dance.

D. MORGAN

Gallery

'Untitled' — Alison Vincent

'Reefscape' — Jenny Dowde

'Angel' — Bonnie Pierce

Bag collection — Alison Vincent

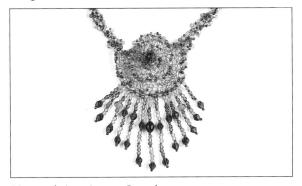

'Cascade' — Jenny Dowde

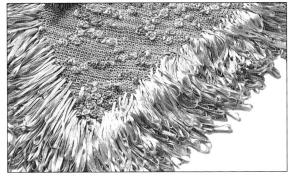

'Bride's Triangular Neckpiece' — Lynne Johnson

'Fire Eyed' —Cris Boerner

'Homage to Magpie' —Jenny Dowde

'Blue Haze' —Jenny Dowde

'Striped Diamonds' —Lynne Johnson

'Outback' —Jenny Dowde

'WhatKnot Vest' —Jenny Dowde